INVESTMENT

THE STUDY OF AN ECONOMIC AGGREGATE

MATHEMATICAL ECONOMICS TEXTS

Editors

K. ARROW, Professor of Economics, Harvard University, U.S.A.

F. HAHN, Professor of Economics, London School of Economics, U.K.

J. JOHNSTON, Professor of Econometrics, University of Manchester, U.K.

R. M. SOLOW, Professor of Economics, Massachusetts Institute of Technology, U.S.A.

Students of mathematical economics and econometrics have two unnecessary difficulties. One is that much of what they have to read is spread over the journals, often written in different notations. The second is that the theoretical and the empirical writings often make little reference to each other, and the student is left to relate them.

The main object of this series is to overcome these difficulties. Most of the books are concerned with specific topics in economic theory, but they relate the theory to relevant empirical work. Others deal with the necessary mathematical apparatus of economic theory and econometrics. They are designed for third-year undergraduates and postgraduate students.

The editors are drawn from both sides of the Atlantic and are people who are known both for their contribution to economics and for the emphasis they place on clear exposition.

Titles in the series

Other titles are in preparation

INVESTMENT
THE STUDY OF AN ECONOMIC AGGREGATE

PHILIP J. LUND

OLIVER & BOYD
EDINBURGH
HOLDEN DAY
SAN FRANCISCO . CALIFORNIA

ISBN 0-8162-5405-2
Library of Congress Catalog Card No. 74-159288

First published 1971
© 1971 Philip J. Lund
All rights reserved

Copublished by
OLIVER & BOYD
Tweeddale Court
14 High Street
Edinburgh EH1 1YL
A Division of Longman Group Limited
and HOLDEN DAY INC.
500 Sansome Street
San Francisco, California

Printed in the United States of America

PREFACE

Fixed investment plays a major role in economic growth and cyclical fluctuations, and is the subject of much previous and current research. Yet no single volume describes its role, discusses the theories attempting to explain its determination, and examines the methods and results of its empirical investigation. This text, written particularly for first-year undergraduate and graduate students, is designed to fill that gap.

The text results from my own study of fixed investment in the United Kingdom. My Ph.D. Thesis, accepted by the University of Manchester in 1969, was an econometric study of investment in industrial buildings and machine tools during 1948–66. Earlier work, published in Oxford Economic Papers and The Manchester School, had investigated pre-war investment and variations in the gestation lags of capital goods. I am grateful to the authors of The Manchester School for permission to reproduce much of that article in this text.

Particular thanks are due to Professor J. Johnston who encouraged the writing of both my thesis and this text. Thanks are also due to him and D. Todd for helpful comments on an earlier draft. Other valuable comments and advice have been received from various people, especially Professor J. Parry Lewis. The typing of the manuscript was kindly organised by Mrs H. M. Hall. Miss P. A. Bennett carefully prepared the figures and assisted with the calculations. Finally, my wife has provided constant assistance with the burden of proof-reading.

Since the text was first written, a number of further contributions to both the theory and empirical investigation of investment have been published. Publishing, like investment, is subject to lags and no text can hope fully to keep pace with the research. Rather than out-dating this text, the recent contributions stress the continuing importance of the topic and the necessity for all serious students of economics to acquaint themselves with it.

Wendover   P.J.L.
Bucks.

44069

CONTENTS

Chapter 1

INTRODUCTION

1.1. Types of Investment

Investment may be defined as the sacrifice of current consumption possibilities in the hope of realising increased consumption possibilities in the future. It is a flow variable—the rate of addition to the stock of wealth, capital, which has been accumulated in the past with this hope of increasing future consumption possibilities. Investment may be measured in either net or gross terms. Gross investment is the sum of the additions to the capital stock. Net investment is the sum of these additions minus any reductions in the existing stock of capital.

Investment may be undertaken by individuals, firms, or by government. It may also take many forms; five separate classes of investment are identified below:

   (i)   in human potential,

   (ii) in intangible assets,

   (iii) in financial assets,

   (iv) in stocks and work in progress,

   (v) in fixed assets.

Both individuals and the community as a whole invest in various forms of human potential, which although they are not always tangible nor easily quantifiable and thus measurable, are nevertheless of significant importance in an assessment of an individual's or community's current and expected future material welfare. For example, a nation may invest in its population, both current and future, by the provision of educational and medical services; in its capacity for economic growth by the development of technical knowledge; and in its 'national heritage'

1

by the fostering of a cultural, economic, social and legal environment conducive to human happiness and welfare.

The acquisition of intangible assets such as patents, copyrights and 'goodwill' are considered as investments by the individuals or firms which obtain them, and their value is often estimated by accountants. However, national income accounts do not attempt to measure either the value of, or the value of changes in these assets. In so far as these assets represent the intangible advantages of particular firms vis-a-vis their competitors within an economy, an investment in them by one firm may correspond to a loss of advantage by other firms, and hence their total value for the economy as a whole may be relatively small.

The acquisition of financial assets, such as company shares or government bonds, is an act of investment by the purchaser. However, an important feature of financial assets is that they are always exactly balanced by corresponding liabilities. Thus a company share is an asset to its holder, but a liability to the company which issued it; similarly a government bond is an asset to its holder but also constitutes part of a national debt. This two-sided nature of financial assets[1] means that in a closed economy (i.e. one that does not engage in economic activities with the rest of the world) the economy's net financial assets must always equal zero: for each financial asset held there is a corresponding and equal liability. It follows that net financial investment in the economy as a whole must be zero: each increase (decrease) in assets being matched by an equal increase (decrease) in liabilities.[2] If, however, the assumption of a closed economy is relaxed—economic activities being undertaken with the rest of the world—net financial investment (or disinvestment) becomes possible for the economy as a whole, and is defined as the increase (decrease) in its net claims on the rest of the world. Net financial investment, so defined, is recorded in national income accounts.

A firm undertakes investment when it purchases a good which is expected to yield a productive service for some length of time in the future. As all goods have some finite expected life span the classification of expenditures into current and capital is essentially arbitrary. However, the following guidelines have been laid down by the Statistical Office of the United Nations:[3]

1 Both deposits held by commercial banks and other financial institutions, and currency (notes and coin) also possess this two-sided nature. A bank deposit is an asset to the depositor, but a liability to the bank; and currency is an asset to its holder, but a liability to the issuing authority.

2 Net financial investment (disinvestment) is, of course, possible by particular individuals or groups within the economy.

3 United Nations (1964), p. 28.

'Gross fixed capital formation includes the value of the purchases and own-account construction of fixed assets (land, civilian construction and works, machinery and equipment) by enterprises, private-non-profit institutions in their capacity as landlords and general government . . . As a general rule all durable producers' goods with an expected lifetime of more than one year, which accordingly are not entirely written off in the accounts of the year in which they are purchased, should be included. In practice, however, it is convenient to exclude from capital formation and to charge to current expense, small items, many of which will be recurrent, such as expenditure on hand tools, motor tyres, office desk equipment and the like, irrespective of their lifetime. In particular this is the case with those goods which most enterprises would customarily charge to current expense.

'A similar problem arises as regards the treatment of expenditures on repair and maintenance. In principle, expenditure on repairs over and above what is needed to keep the capital goods in a state of constant repair should be included. As a practical solution, however, it will often only be possible to include instead the costs of major alterations and renewals. Thus, even repairs which involve the replacement of durable parts with a lifetime longer than one year will generally have to be excluded.'

The broad categories of goods which are classified as fixed capital assets are buildings, civil engineering works, and machinery and vehicles (other than for private use). In the case of existing fixed assets, each purchase must be exactly matched by a corresponding sale, and thus within a closed economy, aggregate investment in fixed assets must take the form of the creation of new fixed assets. If the assumption of a closed economy is relaxed, investment (or disinvestment) in existing fixed assets becomes possible for the economy as a whole; residents may buy or sell existing fixed assets in other economies, and similarly non-residents may buy or sell such assets in the home economy. However, because of the nature of most fixed capital assets, international transactions in them are rare.

Investment in fixed assets is undertaken by both individuals and government as well as by firms. The purchase of a dwelling is considered to be an act of investment, and so the construction of new dwellings constitutes a part of national investment in fixed assets. However, although consumer durables, such as private motor cars, televisions, and refrigerators, may have an expected lifetime of several years, they are not treated as fixed assets for the purposes of national income accounting. Government investment in fixed assets may take the form of the building of schools, roads and hospitals, the provision of new public housing, and the construction of new government offices. Public corporations (nationalised industries) also undertake investment in fixed assets, for example in electric power plant, reservoirs and airports.

This text examines the determinants of that part of national gross fixed investment which is undertaken by the private (non-government) sector, excluding the purchase of new dwellings. In United Kingdom statistical terminology, this may be referred to as 'private-sector non-dwelling gross fixed capital formation'; in the United States, as 'gross private fixed non-residential domestic investment'. The following sections of this chapter examine some of the characteristics of this type of investment, especially in the United Kingdom and the United States and discuss its role in both economic growth and cyclical fluctuations.

1.2. Investment in the United Kingdom, 1900–67

Statistical information on net financial investment, investment in stocks and work in progress and investment in fixed assets in the United Kingdom is published in the national income and expenditure accounts prepared by the Central Statistical Office. The following tables utilise this and other available information to present the trends in, and composition of, investment in the United Kingdom during the period 1900–67.

Table 1.1 presents estimates of net financial investment abroad, of the value of the increase in stocks and work in progress, and of gross and net domestic fixed capital formation during the periods 1900–14, 1920–29, 1930–38, 1946–51, 1952–57, 1958–62 and 1963–67; all estimates being at current prices. In the calculation of total investment, as both financial investment abroad and the value of the increase in stocks and work in progress are measured in net terms, domestic fixed capital formation has also been included in net terms. Net domestic fixed capital formation is calculated by subtracting an estimate of capital consumption from the figure for gross domestic fixed capital formation; the estimate of capital consumption being calculated on the basis of the age distribution of the existing capital stock.[4] In the last column, total (net) investment is expressed as a percentage of national income; national income being used as the denominator in preference to gross national product because it is the net income concept corresponding to the net investment concept used in the numerator. National income is calculated by subtracting the estimate of capital consumption from gross national product. The main features of the trends in investment shown in table 1.1 are the post-war increase in the importance of stock-

---

4 For a description of the methods involved, and their application to United Kingdom data, see Redfern (1955), Dean (1964), and Central Statistical Office (1968), pp. 383–387.

TABLE 1.1

United Kingdom investment and national income, 1900–67 (average annual rates): £ million, current market prices

	Net financial investment abroad	Value of physical increase in stocks and work in progress	Gross domestic fixed capital formation	Capital consumption	Net domestic fixed capital formation	Total (net) investment	National income	Total (net) investment as % of national income
1900–14	+121	+14	161	106	+55	+190	1917	9·9
1920–29	+97	+21	406	299	+107	+225	3967	5·7
1930–38	−26	+23	457	313	+144	+141	4123	3·4
1946–51	−24	+125	1452	893	+559	+660	9867	6·7
1952–57	+118	+171	2722	1434	+1288	+1577	15219	10·4
1958–62	+66	+254	4140	1966	+2174	+2494	20939	11·9
1963–67	−154	+327	6168	2718	+3468	+3641	28270	12·9

Sources: 1900–38—London and Cambridge Economic Service (1967), except for the figure for net financial investment abroad, which incorporates estimates for 1901–13 published in British National Export Council (1968).

1946–67—Successive issues of the annual Central Statistical Office publication, National Income and Expenditure.

building and the ever increasing magnitude of fixed capital formation. Although a substantial part of this latter increase simply reflects the effect of inflation on capital goods prices, gross domestic fixed capital formation at constant (1958) prices did increase from an annual average rate of £1197 mn to one of £5438 mn between 1900–14 and 1963–67. Total investment has therefore tended to increase, both absolutely and also as a proportion of national income, especially in the post World War II period. The table also reveals the increasing importance of domestic fixed capital formation vis-a-vis financial investment abroad during the period 1900–67.

The composition of gross domestic fixed capital formation by type of asset during 1920–67 is shown in table 1.2. The percentage of gross domestic fixed capital formation which consisted of investment in dwellings was much higher (over 30%) in the inter-war period than in the post-war period (about 20%); consequently the non-dwelling component of gross fixed capital formation increased more rapidly during the period 1920–67 than did the total. Other features shown by the table are the marked increase in the share of investment in plant and machinery and the comparative long-run stability in the shares of investment in vehicles (excluding ships) and in building and works. The shares of these broadly defined asset groups in gross domestic fixed capital formation are now (approximately): vehicles, 10%; plant and machinery, 40%; dwellings, 20%; new building and works, 30%.

Table 1.3 shows the composition of non-dwelling gross fixed capital formation by sector during 1920–67. No more detailed division is available for the inter-war years than that between the public and private sectors. For the purpose of the original statistical information, the public sector in these years was defined to include the public utilities of electricity, gas, water supply and railways, although some of these were at that time under private ownership. It is therefore difficult to draw conclusions about the long-term trends in the relative shares of the public and private sectors in non-dwelling gross fixed capital formation. During the post-war period, the share of the personal sector (one-man businesses and partnerships) has fallen dramatically, that of companies and government remained relatively stable, and that of the public corporations increased. Of non-dwelling gross fixed capital formation, about 5% is now undertaken by the personal sector, about 50% by companies, about 25% by the public corporations, and about 20% by government.

The industrial composition of non-dwelling gross fixed capital formation is shown in table 1.4. The most evident trend is the very large decline in the share of transport and communication since the beginning

TABLE 1.2

Composition of United Kingdom gross domestic fixed capital formation by
type of asset: 1920–67 (percentages)

	Road vehicles	Railway rolling stock	Ships	Aircraft	Total vehicles	Plant and machinery	Dwellings	Other new buildings and works
1920–29	8·1	2·5	7·4	—	18·0	26·2	27·3	28·5
1930–38	9·2	1·5	2·5	—	13·2	26·4	33·8	26·6
1947–51	9·4	1·8	4·5	0·5	16·2	37·2	20·7	25·9
1952–57	7·1	2·0	3·6	0·7	13·4	37·0	22·4	27·2
1958–62	7·4	2·0	3·7	0·8	13·9	37·4	17·9	30·8
1963–67	6·9	0·6	1·9	0·5	9·9	38·5	20·1	31·5

Sources: 1920–38—Feinstein (1965), table 3.31. The percentages are based on estimates of gross domestic fixed capital formation by type of asset, at 1930 market prices.
1947–66—Successive issues of National Income and Expenditure. The percentages are based on estimates at current market prices, and the transfer costs of land and buildings have been included in new buildings and works.

TABLE 1.3

Composition of United Kingdom non-dwelling gross fixed capital formation
by sector: 1920–67 (percentages)

	Private sector			Public sector			
	Personal	Companies	Total	Public companies	Central government	Local government	Total
1920–29	..	..	59·5	..	..	..	40·5
1930–38	..	..	51·0	..	..	..	49·0
1948–51	15·2	45·6	60·8	19·7	8·7	10·8	39·2
1952–57	10·5	44·8	55·3	24·0	9·4	11·3	44·7
1958–62	7·6	50·8	58·4	23·3	6·7	11·6	41·6
1963–67	5·6	48·1	53·7	25·9	5·8	14·6	46·3

Sources: 1920–38—Feinstein (1965), p. 3.34. The percentages are based on estimates of gross domestic fixed
capital formation by sector, at 1930 market prices.
1948–67—Successive issues of National Income and Expenditure. The percentages are based on
estimates at current market prices.

TABLE 1.4

Composition of United Kingdom non-dwelling gross fixed capital formation
by industry: 1900–67 (percentages)

	Fuel, power and water	Transport and communication	Public services	Manufacturing	Distribution, finance, agriculture, etc.
1900–14	..	40·3	..	..	..
1920–29	16·8	32·5	10·6	24·8	15·3
1930–38	22·1	21·1	16·1	23·9	16·8
1948–51	16·2	16·1	9·5	31·6	23·1
1952–57	18·3	14·6	10·3	33·0	21·7
1958–62	16·2	14·5	12·5	30·7	22·2
1963–67	18·4	10·7	15·7	26·1	24·0

Sources: 1900–38—London and Cambridge Economic Service (1967).
1948–67—Successive issues of National Income and Expenditure. The industrial estimates include the
transfer costs of land and buildings for 1900–38, but do not do so for 1948–67; hence for
these latter years the sum of the industrial percentages is slightly less than 100%. The percentages are based on estimates at current market prices.

of the century. Manufacturing industry and the public utilities have accounted for a fairly steady proportion of the total, whilst the share going to the provision of publicly-provided services has increased rapidly in the post-war period. Amongst the remaining industrial groups, the share of the distributive and service trades has been rising to around 18 %, whilst that of agriculture has fallen steadily to about 3 %.

As shown in table 1.1, net investment has accounted for an increasing proportion of national income, at least since 1930. Similarly gross domestic fixed capital formation has tended to become an increasing proportion of gross national product (national income + capital consumption) during this period. Moreover, it has been a particularly volatile component. Table 1.5 shows the annual percentage changes in each main expenditure component during the post-war period 1948–67 classified by magnitude of the change. The changes were calculated on the basis of constant-price data, and hence reflect changes in the volume of expenditure rather than merely the effects of price changes. The table clearly reveals the relative constancy of gross national product and consumers expenditure as compared with the other expenditure categories. Gross domestic fixed capital formation has shown the most sizeable annual increases, and the table reveals the private-sector non-dwelling component of it to be particularly volatile. Both of these factors make a study of its determination vital to any proper understanding of the recent performance of the United Kingdom economy.

1.3. Investment in the United States, 1929–67

An analysis of the annual real percentage changes in each main expenditure category of United States gross national product reveals a rather less striking picture. Although the figures presented in table 1.6 show gross private domestic investment to be much more volatile than either gross national product or personal consumption expenditures, it appears little more so than government purchases, exports or imports. Moreover, the actual range of variation is greater in these other three categories than in gross private domestic investment. However special factors, especially the Korean and Vietnam wars, account for most of the larger variations in government expenditures, whilst exports and imports, though volatile, are quantitatively relatively unimportant in the United States economy. Another factor of importance is that United States national income accounts include the relatively stable government fixed investment in 'government purchases of goods and services' rather than in 'gross fixed capital formation' as is the United Kingdom (and standard United Nations) practice. On the other hand, the U.S.

TABLE 1.5

Annual real percentage changes in each expenditure component of United Kingdom gross national product (and imports), classified by magnitude of change: 1948/9–66/67

Number of annual percentage changes

	Increases of more than 10%	Increases of between 5% and 10%	Increases of less than 5%	Decreases of less than 5%	Decreases of more' than 5%
Consumers expenditure	—	—	17	2	—
Public authorities current expenditure	1	3	10	5	—
Gross domestic fixed capital formation	2	9	7	1	—
Exports	2	3	10	4	—
Imports	2	6	9	1	1
Gross national product	—	1	17	1	—
Private sector non-dwelling gross domestic fixed capital formation	6	2	5	4	2

Source: Based on constant (1958) market price data obtained from successive issues of National Income and Expenditure.

TABLE 1.6

Annual real percentage changes in each expenditure component of United States gross national product (and imports), classified by magnitude of change: 1946/47–66/67

	Number of annual percentage changes				
	Increases of more than 10%	Increases of between 5% and 10%	Increases of less than 5%	Decreases of less than 5%	Decreases of more than 5%
Personal consumption expenditure	—	6	15	—	—
Government purchases of goods and services	6	4	7	2	2
Gross private domestic investment	6	2	3	5	5
Exports	6	4	6	1	4
Imports	6	5	4	4	2
Gross national product	—	8	10	3	—
Gross private fixed non-residential domestic investment	5	7	3	4	2

Source: Based on constant market (1958) price data obtained from the 1967 edition of the biennial Department of Commerce publication, Business Statistics, and subsequent issues of the Survey of Current Business.

total 'gross private domestic investment' includes the highly volatile element 'change in business inventories'. However, table 1.6 does show gross private fixed nonresidential domestic investment to be that component of gross national product which shows the most consistent sizeable increases, and yet to be particularly volatile. It appears that this economic aggregate may play an important role in the determination of United States growth and cyclical fluctuations.

The increase in United States domestic investment during 1929–67 is clearly shown in table 1.7. The total was particularly low during the depression years of the early 1930's, and also during World War II. In 1932 gross private domestic investment was a mere $1·0bn, representing only 1·7% of gross national product in that year. In 1933, fixed nonresidential private investment was less than a quarter of its 1929 level! Since the war, total private domestic investment, and especially its fixed nonresidential component, has expanded considerably. Even after allowing for price increases, this component increased by almost 80% between 1946–51 and 1963–67; from $36·0bn to $64·7bn at constant (1958) market prices. In the latter period, investment (as defined on p. 4) accounted for 10·2% of United States gross national product, compared to only 7·5% in the United Kingdom.

The industrial composition of United States gross private fixed nonresidential domestic investment can be seen by examining the series on new plant and equipment expenditures'. This series differs from that presented in the first column of table 1.7 in that it excludes investment 'by farmers, professionals, institutions and real estate firms, and also certain outlays normally charged to current account. Table 1.8 summarises its industrial composition during the post-war period. The only clear trend shown is the decline in the share of non-durable manufacturing industry. Unlike that in the United Kingdom, the share of transport and communication in fixed investment has remained constant during the post-war period. Even after allowing for the exclusion of government and agriculture from this series, the shares of manufacturing and transport and communication appear higher in the United States than in the United Kingdom, whilst that of the general service sector seems lower.

The total of United States domestic fixed capital formation, including that by government, is presented in United Nations statistics. The total for 1958–66, and its composition by asset, is shown in table 1.9. This shows the share of dwellings to have been falling, whilst that of machinery has been rising. Compared with the United Kingdom situation, more of United States fixed investment takes the form of non-dwelling construction and less takes the form of machinery.

TABLE 1.7

United States domestic investment and gross national product, 1929–67 (average annual rates): $ billion, current market prices

	Gross private domestic investment				Gross national product	Gross private domestic investment as % of gross national product
	Fixed non-residential	Residential	Change in business inventories	Total		
1929–38	5·5	1·7	−0·1	7·1	77·8	9·1
1939–45	7·3	2·4	0·9	10·5	155·2	6·8
1946–51	25·4	13·8	4·1	43·3	261·2	16·6
1952–57	37·9	20·0	2·3	60·3	388·9	15·5
1958–62	46·8	23·4	3·0	73·1	503·0	14·5
1963–67	70·3	26·1	8·4	104·9	689·0	15·2

Source: The 1967 edition of Business Statistics, and subsequent issues of the Survey of Current Business.

TABLE 1.8

Composition of United States new plant and equipment expenditures by industry: 1946–67 (percentages)

	Manufacturing industry		Transport and communication (including rail)	Public utilities and mining	Commercial and other (including trade, services, finance, construction)
	Durable	Non-durable			
1946–51	17·0	23·8	17·5	15·7	26·0
1952–57	20·5	21·7	16·1	18·9	22·8
1958–62	18·6	20·3	16·9	19·6	24·6
1963–67	21·8	20·9	16·1	18·9	22·3

Source: The 1967 edition of Business Statistics, and subsequent issues of the Survey of Current Business. The percentages are based on estimates at current market prices.

TABLE 1.9

Composition of United States gross domestic fixed capital formation by type of asset: 1958–66

| | Gross domestic fixed capital formation at current market prices (annual rates) | Asset composition (percentages) | | | | |
		Dwellings	Non-residential buildings	Other construction and works	Transport equipment	Machinery and other
1958–62	85·6	29·0	17·9	19·2	9·6	24·3
1963–66	114·0	24·2	19·7	18·1	11·0	27·0

Source: The 1967 edition of the United Nations Yearbook of National Accounts Statistics. The percentages are based on estimates at current market prices.

1.4. Fixed Investment and Economic Growth

Fixed nonresidential investment, along with such factors as the growth of the labour force and the advancement of technical knowledge, has long been considered an important determinant of a nation's potential rate of economic growth. This is because such fixed investment raises the amount of productive capital available per person employed, and thus raises aggregate productive potential. Post-war experience has provided support for the view that a high proportion of national resources devoted to fixed investment is a necessary condition for fast economic growth. In particular Japan, which has steadily increased the percentage of its G.N.P. devoted to gross domestic fixed investment to over 30%, has achieved an average annual rate of increase of gross national product during 1950–66 of 9·3%. On the other hand, the United Kingdom and the United States which have used much less than 20% of their G.N.P. in this manner have achieved overall growth rates of only about 3% and 4% respectively.

Denison (1967) has recently attempted to measure the contributions of several different factors to the recorded economic growth of nine western countries. His estimates are based on the assumption that[5]

'for all producing units, the tendency toward proportionality of factor prices and marginal products under conditions of reasonably high employment is sufficiently strong in the United States and . . . in Western Europe for distributive shares to provide an adequate basis for analysis of the relative contributions of the various factors to growth.'

The estimates of the contribution of each factor input were obtained by multiplying the growth rate of the input by its average share of national income. The results, with respect to the capital input 'nonresidential structures and equipment' are summarised in table 1.10. Increased inputs of this factor are shown to account for between 9 and 20% of the growth rates of the nine countries examined. Of the twenty-three different sources of growth which were considered, increased input of nonresidential structures and equipment was the most important in one country (Norway), the second in another (Germany), the third in three (Denmark, Netherlands, Norway), and the fourth in another three (United States, Belgium, France). Of the other sources of growth considered, only 'advances of knowledge' was found to play a more important role. Moreover, separate examination of the latter and more normal part of the period, 1955–62, increased the relative importance of nonresdential structures and equipment as a source of growth.

5 Denison (1967), p. 35.

TABLE 1.10

Denison's estimate of contribution of fixed investment
to growth of total national income in nine western countries, 1950–62

| | Growth rate of total national income (%) | Contribution to growth rate of: | | | Percentage of growth due to increased stock of non-residential structures and equipment |
		Increased total factor input	Non-residential structures and equipment	Increased output per unit of input	
United States	3·32	1·95	0·43	1·37	13
N.W. Europe	4·78	1·69	0·64	3·07	14
Belgium	3·20	1·17	0·39	2·03	13
Denmark	3·51	1·55	0·66	1·96	20
France	4·92	1·24	0·56	3·68	12
Germany	7·26	2·78	1·02	4·48	14
Netherlands	4·73	1·19	0·66	2·82	15
Norway	3·45	1·04	0·79	2·41	23
United Kingdom	2·29	1·11	0·43	1·18	18
Italy	5·96	1·66	0·54	4·30	9

Source: Denison (1967), tables 21.1–21.20.

Although both neoclassical and Keynesian economic theorists considered fixed investment to be an important source of growth, it is only since Keynes that the rate of fixed investment has been widely recognised as a determinant of the observed short-run, or cyclical, fluctuations in real national income.[6] Neoclassical economists considered that when in a state of equilibrium, capitalist economies operate at, or close to, their full-employment and hence potential levels of real national income. Observed departures from this desirable state were considered to be of only a temporary and self-correcting nature. This complacent theoretical position, which was questioned by Continental writers of the late 19th and early 20th centuries such as Wicksell (1898), Tugan-Baranowsky (1901) and Spiethoff (1902) was finally shaken by the prolonged and very severe economic depression which hit all the major economies in the capitalist world in the early 1930's. The harsh realities of this depression prompted a systematic re-examination[7] and attack of the postulates of neoclassical theory, which in turn led to the general acceptance of the notion that the level of aggregate demand in an economy may be insufficient to necessitate producing at, or even close to, the full-employment level of real national income. Unemployment of both men and machines was accepted as being both possible and, unless rectifying action was taken, potentially permanent. The rate of fixed investment came to be recognised as a determinant not only of the potential growth in real national income, but also of the extent to which, at any point in time, the potential level of real national income is attained. These theoretical developments in macro-economics, together with the subsequently accepted responsibility of governments to ensure a high and stable level of employment, have brought about the present-day situation in which governments attempt to influence the rate of fixed investment by means of various fiscal, monetary and direct policy measures. However, effective policies to influence fixed investment can only be designed if the factors determining it—at least at the aggregate level—are properly understood. The remainder of this text discusses various alternative theories of aggregate fixed investment (private, nonresidential), and examines their empirical validity.

The remaining components of aggregate fixed investment are probably of less current economic significance, particularly in the generation of

6 The evolution of academic thought on the nature of business cycles and the role of fixed investment in their generation is well described in Hansen (1951), particularly chs. 13–18.

7 See particularly Keynes (1936), the main innovations of which are described and discussed in Hansen (1953).

cyclical fluctuations and economic growth. Public sector fixed capital formation (both by public corporations and government itself) is determined, in the context of any given economic situation, by an interplay of political pressures. A study of its determination thus falls at least as much within the realm of politics as within that of economics. Moreover, with reference to an understanding of the operation of an economy and in particular how public policy affects an economy, fixed capital formation by the public-sector can be considered as an exogenous variable; that is, one that is imposed on the economic system by those responsible for public policy. Private-sector residential fixed capital formation results from the demand by individuals and families for housing. The level of this demand is likely to be determined by a combination of their own circumstances (e.g. personal incomes, formation of new household units, etc.), the ways in which public policy affects them (e.g., rates of tax on personal incomes and wealth) and the institutional economic environment (e.g., the availability of finance for house-purchase). Some of the factors affecting such capital formation are thus under the direct control, and some under the indirect control, of public policy, whereas some are perhaps only marginally so affected. Moreover, as dwellings have accounted for only a fairly small and declining proportion of total private fixed investment in both the United Kingdom and the United States, it is probably not of too great importance in the determination of the levels of economic activity and employment in these two countries.

The importance of private nonresidential fixed investment in the economic system is reflected by the volume of literature devoted to it. Chapter 2 discusses the alternative theories that have been proposed to explain its determination, and chs. 3–5 examine the techniques and results of different methods of assessing their validity. For sake of brevity, expressions such as 'private nonresidential fixed investment' will be replaced by the terms 'investment' and 'capital expenditure' as appropriate.

Chapter 2

THEORIES OF AGGREGATE INVESTMENT

2.1. The Level of Aggregation

Aggregate investment results from decisions made by individual firms. This important fact raises the question of whether the basis of a theory of aggregate investment should relate to individual firms, or to highly aggregated economic units, such as a particular industry or group of industries. Is the appropriate theory to be derived as the aggregation of some micro theory, or is it a separate macro theory?

In answering this question it is necessary to bear in mind some of the characteristics which a useful and meaningful theory should possess. Firstly, it must be amenable to verification. Although theories concerning unobservable or unmeasurable variables can never be proved wrong, they are unlikely to be of much practical use. The price of generality is imprecision. Secondly, a useful theory is one that lends itself to quantification. Economists—and particularly those concerned with policy issues—not only want to know the directional influence of one variable upon another, but also want to quantify the strength of this influence. For example, although investment theory may correctly state that aggregate investment is negatively related to the rate of interest, those responsible for policy decisions really need an estimate of the quantitative effect of a specific change in interest rates on investment. The theory may be generally valid, but its quantitative importance may differ from country to country and also over time. The quantification of economic theories in specific circumstances is one of the most important roles of econometrics. Thirdly, a useful theory is one that enables predictions to be made about the variable(s) to which it relates. In addition to providing a quantitative estimate of the effects of intentional policy changes, an economic theory should also be able to forecast the effects of changes taking place within the economic system itself. For example, a useful theory of investment should be capable of development to

21

provide forecasts of the effects of changes in such variables as profits and capacity utilisation. Given the volatile nature of aggregate fixed investment, accurate forecasts of its future trends are required by those responsible for adjusting public policy to meet changing economic circumstances.

Bearing these points in mind, three alternative methods of explaining, and hence predicting, aggregate investment can be considered. They are:

  (i) to develop a theory to explain the capital expenditures of individual firms, and hence explain and predict aggregate investment as the sum of these capital expenditures.

 (ii) to develop a theory to explain the capital expenditures of individual firms and then, assuming that it is possible to aggregate this theory to the required level, use it to explain and predict aggregate investment.

(iii) to develop a separate macro theory of aggregate investment, and use it for purposes of explanation and prediction. Such a theory, though not necessarily corresponding exactly to any micro theory, could nevertheless be developed with reference to the hypotheses incorporated in micro theories.

The first of these procedures is not feasible for studying aggregate investment, particularly in the United Kingdom. This is simply because satisfactory data is not available for all firms undertaking capital expenditure. However, even if such data were available, the calculations required would be too burdensome to justify use of the method. Moreover, empirical studies, such as that by Grunfeld and Griliches (1960) of the capital expenditures of eight large U.S. manufacturing corporations, have shown that the proportion of the variation in an economic aggregate explained by a set of identical micro equations may not in practice be as large as that explained by the single corresponding equation relating to the aggregate. Hence, although this procedure would provide a clear insight into the factors influencing the investment decisions of individual firms, it may not be the best method for explaining and subsequently predicting aggregate capital expenditure.

The second of the proposed procedures is the one which is usually adopted. It has been aptly described by Eisner and Strotz (1963).[1]

'Starting with first principles pertaining to the decision-making process of the firm, it (economics) should proceed to a quantitative statement of the influence of major social changes on the total amount of investment undertaken in an economy. This probably constitutes the common framework into which most investigators in this area feel their contributions must ultimately

1 Eisner and Strotz, p. 61.

fit. We begin at the micro level and in the arm chair. We postulate, as pure hypothesis, the principles which guide decision-making units, which in this case are firms, in deciding upon their investment policies. We specify carefully the constraints, technological, financial, and organisational, which condition the choices actually made; and by careful use of logic we derive significant qualitative propositions regarding how investment decisions are affected by changes in the parameters that define the opportunities open to the firm. Once having articulated the theory of investment at the level of the individual firm, we then imagine that we may proceed synthetically to deduce relationships among broad economic aggregates which govern the investment desires of the business sector as a whole. Firmly rooted in micro theory, a macro theory thus emerges.'

The obvious weakness in this procedure is the transformation from the micro theory to the macro theory—the aggregation step. Theil (1954) has shown that if a micro-level relationship is aggregated to the macro-level by simply defining each of the macro variables as the sum (or average) of the corresponding micro variables, then estimation of the resulting aggregate relationships using ordinary least-squares yields biased estimates of the underlying micro-parameters. Moreover Boot and de Wit (1960) have shown that this bias can be fairly substantial. Thus, although a postulated relationship may be perfectly valid at the individual firm level, statistical testing of it at the macro level may lead to its rejection. The parameters of the macro relationship correspond to the parameters of the underlying micro relationship only if the macro variables are defined as the geometric mean of the corresponding micro variables. Unfortunately economic data are not published in geometric mean form, nor are all the micro observations usually available to permit the calculation of such means. Moreover, there are other criticisms of this aggregation step. Variables which appear to be of importance at the micro level may be unimportant at the macro level, and vice-versa. Competitive forces within an industry, and the desire to maintain a firm's share of its potential market are often mentioned by businessmen as factors inducing investment,[2] yet to a large extent these factors will cancel out at the aggregate level. On the other hand, some variables, particularly such public policy variables as interest rates and tax allowances affect all firms in the same direction; thus, even though they may appear unimportant to individual firms, they may play an important role in determining aggregate investment.

The third procedure suggested, that of developing a separate macro theory to predict macro behaviour, has been recommended by Peston (1959). He argued that 'economic theory at any level of aggregation

2 See, for example, Barna (1962).

exists on a par with economic theory at any other level'[3] and that the attempt to derive macro-relationships in such a way that they are consistent with micro-relationships 'leaves macro theory somehow subsidiary to micro theory'.[4] His arguments imply that it is possible to have two separate theories of investment—one to explain the capital expenditures of individual firms, the other to explain aggregate capital expenditure. Unfortunately Peston did not proffer any advice on how separate macro theories might be constructed. Ultimately, recourse must surely be made to a consideration of the decision-making processes which between them result in aggregate capital expenditure, and hence to a theory or theories about the behaviour of micro units. But the arguments of Peston do suggest that an acceptable macro theory need not have an exact correspondence with some accepted micro theory. This conclusion is of particular relevance if alternative theories are to be tested using econometric methods. It has already been argued that the ranking of variables according to their importance in the explanation of capital expenditure may well be different for macro and micro explanations. Since econometric methods are only able to cope satisfactorily with a limited number of explanatory variables, the variables chosen to be included in regressions to explain and predict aggregate capital expenditure may well be different from those included in regressions to explain and predict the capital expenditures of individual firms. Although the following section discusses theories of investment which are usually expounded in macro-terms, they are seen to be empirically arid. Recourse must therefore be taken to theories relating more particularly to the behaviour of individual firms. These are discussed in sections 3–8.

2.2. Innovation and Autonomous Investment

A distinction is sometimes made between two types of investment—autonomous and induced. Autonomous investment results from new inventions, discoveries, products and processes, which are considered to occur at a rate which is independent of such economic variables as the flow of profits or the rate of interest. Such investment is likely to lead to a growth in national income, which in turn may induce further investment, thus known as induced investment. The concept of autonomous investment is closely associated with that of the innovation process; that of induced investment with that of the acceleration principle (to be discussed in ch. 2 § 5).

3 Peston (1959), p. 59.
4 ibid., p. 59.

The volume of autonomous investment basically depends upon the growth impulses inherent in technological developments. Schumpeter, in various works,[5] has argued that whereas invention may proceed at a uniform rate, innovation is likely to proceed in marked cycles of activity and inactivity. Technological break-throughs do not occur at regular intervals; they appear 'discontinuously in groups or swarms'.[6] This irregularity is intensified by the herdlike characteristics of entrepreneurs; they will continue to conduct their activities in a conventional way until one of them introduces a new procedure which, if successful, compels the others to follow. Whenever 'the trade beholds the new thing done and its major problems solved, it becomes much easier for other people to do the same thing and even to improve upon it'.[7] Eventually, a halt is called to the rush of innovations, since the new innovations cannot be incorporated into the existing economic system without an intervening period of readjustment; this process is, according to Schumpeter, the essence of the recession.

This theory of innovation implies a theory of investment, since innovation involves capital expenditure, 'which accordingly is not distributed evenly in time, but appears en masse at intervals'.[8] However, the difficulty with this simple theory is that it does not lend itself to quantification or prediction. Klein (1966) has commented:[9]

'this theory maintains that the demand for producer goods depends upon subjective anticipations regarding future markets, technological developments, population growth, and various other uncertain forces about which the economist has no adequate theory.'

Moreover, the Schumpeterian theory ignores such economic considerations as the cost of the factors required to produce capital goods and the expected profits to be derived from them. It is divorced from any theory of utility maximisation on the part of firms, and in particular from the classically accepted doctrine of profit maximisation. It is to theories based on these objectives to which attention is now turned.

2.3. The Neoclassical Theory of Capital Accumulation

The foundations of capital theory were stated by Fisher in The Theory of Interest (1930). According to this theory capital is simply

5 See, for example, The Theory of Economic Development (1934) and Business Cycles (1939).
6 Schumpeter (1934), p. 223.
7 Schumpeter (1939), p. 100.
8 ibid., pp. 87–88.
9 Klein (1966), p. 62.

future income discounted to the present. Capital goods have value only because they are expected to yield a flow of services (income) in the future, and that value is determined by discounting the value of this flow of income to the present. Discounting is necessary because individuals are impatient and have a preference for present rather than future enjoyment; the rate at which an individual will discount certain future income being given by his rate of time preference. The theory states that the size of the capital stock and the rate of interest are mutually determined by the supply and demand for capital services, both of which are expressed as a function of the rate of interest. The fundamental features of this theory have been summarised by Kuh (1963a);[10]

'It is a theory at the level of microeconomic choice and at the level of total market price determination which has the major ingredients, correctly related to each other, that a capital theory should have. The fundamental ingredients are the productivity of capital and thrift. The opportunity to profit from capital requires the sacrifice of present for future income on terms reflected by the market rate of interest. This is an equilibrium theory of capital.'

Keynes (1936) expounded a theory of investment which is analogous to Fisher's theory of capital. This theory involves the construction of the marginal efficiency of capital, or investment-demand, schedule. Keynes defined the marginal efficiency of a particular capital-asset as 'that rate of discount which would make the present value of the series of annuities given by the returns expected from the capital-asset during its life just equal to its supply price'.[11] Thus, if C is the cost of a capital good with an expected lifetime of n years, $R_1, R_2 \ldots R_n$ is the series of expected annual returns (annuities), the marginal efficiency of the investment, r, is given by

$$C = \frac{R_1}{(1+r)} + \frac{R_2}{(1+r)^2} + \ldots + \frac{R_n}{(1+r)^n} \qquad (2.1)$$

Only if r exceeds the rate of interest, i, will it be profitable to purchase the capital good.

On the basis of this definition of the marginal efficiency of a particular capital-asset, Keynes proceeded to describe a schedule relating the rate of aggregate investment to the correspondingly marginal efficiency of capital in general which that rate of investment will establish: he called this the investment demand-schedule. Given the rate of interest, the rate of investment is now determined, since 'the rate of investment will be pushed to the point on the investment demand-schedule where the

10 Kuh (1963a), p. 260.
11 Keynes (1936), p. 135.

marginal efficiency of capital in general is equal to the market rate of interest . . . It follows that the inducement to invest depends partly on the investment demand-schedule and partly on the rate of interest'.[12]

Keynes' presentation of the theory of investment has been subject to much criticism. In particular he has been accused of confusing the theory of investment with the theory of capital. Many economists argue that these represent two clearly distinct problems. A theory of capital should seek to explain the determinants of the optimum and thus equilibrium stock of capital for a firm and an economy, whilst a theory of investment should explain the rate of adjustment in those disequilibrium situations in which the capital stock is not at its optimum level. The criticism is that by itself, the neoclassical theory of capital does not provide a satisfactory theory of investment, since no basis is provided for determining the speed of adjustment of the capital stock from one equilibrium situation to another. An example of the strength of feeling on this issue is provided by the writing of Haavelmo (1960):[13]

'I do not . . . reject the possibility that an empirical relation may be found between the rate of interest and the rate of investment. What we should reject is the naive reasoning that there is a "demand schedule" for investment which could be derived from a classical scheme of producers' behaviour in maximising profit. The demand for investment cannot simply be derived from the demand for capital. Demand for a finite addition to the stock of capital can lead to any rate of investment, from almost zero to infinity, depending on the additional hypothesis we introduce regarding the speed of reaction of the capital-users. I think that the sooner this naive, and unfounded theory of the demand-for-investment schedule is abandoned, the sooner we shall have a chance of making some real progress in constructing more powerful theories to deal with the capricious short-run variations in the rate of private investment.'

More recently Jorgenson has pointed out that Haavelmo's criticism is based on an attempt to analyse the demand for capital services by means of comparative statics, and noted that an alternative interpretation is possible:[14]

'Under the hypothesis that the firm is following an optimal path of capital accumulation and that the optimal path is continuous, the initial level of capital services is always equal to the demand for capital services. By imposing this condition at the outset, the demand for investment goods as a function of the rate of interest at any point in time may be analysed by means of comparative dynamics, that is, by comparing alternative paths of capital accumulation, each identical up to that point in time and each continuous at that point.'

12 ibid, pp. 136–137.
13 Haavelmo (1960), p. 216.
14 Jorgenson (1967), p. 148.

A second point of controversy concerning Keynes' presentation has centred around his concept of the marginal efficiency of capital. Keynes claimed that this is identical with Fisher's concept of 'the rate of return over cost'. He quoted Fisher as defining the rate of return over cost as 'that rate which, employed in computing the present worth of all the costs and the present worth of all the returns, will make these two equal'.[15] However, as pointed out by Alchian (1955), Keynes neglected the fact that Fisher's rate of return over cost concept was 'developed in order to rank investment alternatives by the universally correct criterion of maximum present value (and) can be defined only by reference to at least two alternative investment options'.[16] In support of this view he quoted the following two sentences which had been neglected by Keynes:[17]

'Or, as a mathematician would prefer to put it, the rate which, employed in computing the present worth of the whole series of differences between the two income streams (some differences being positive and others negative) will make the total zero. If the rate, so computed, were taken for every possible pair of income streams, compared as to their advantages and disadvantages, it would authentically decide in each case which of the two is to be preferred.'

On the other hand in later chapters of The Theory of Interest, Fisher used the rate of return over cost in contexts which seem to preclude the comparison of two alternative investment opportunities.[18] Moreover, as Alchian admitted, any difference between the Keynesian and Fisherian concepts is irrelevant to the fundamental proposition that the slope of the aggregate investment function is negative:[19]

'Whether one uses the internal rate of return or the Fisherian rate of return over cost to rank investment options according to present net wealth, lower market rates of interest imply larger rates of investment. The fact that his derivation of the negative slope did not correspond to Fisher's led to no difficulty in Keynes' General Theory. How one derives a proposition is irrelevant if one is interested only in the empirical validity of the proposition.'

Fisher and Keynes were indeed in unison in stating that the rate of interest is a crucial determinant of the level of investment. Indeed a similar theory had been expounded much earlier by Wicksell (1898) who suggested that an expansion of investment in fixed capital goods 'will

15 Fisher (1930), p. 168.
16 Alchian (1955), p. 938.
17 Fisher (1930), pp. 168–169.
18 See, for example, the quotation on p. 29.
19 Alchian (1955), p. 942.

take place when their earnings increase or when the rate of interest falls, so that their capital value now exceeds their cost of reproduction'.[20]

However, in order to develop a comprehensive theory of investment it is necessary to consider not only the intersection between, say, Keynes' marginal efficiency of capital schedule and the rate of interest, but also to consider the determinants of the shape and position of the marginal efficiency schedule itself. Wicksell regarded technical discoveries and growth of population as dynamic factors which tend to raise the rate of return on investment. Fisher agreed that the effect of every important discovery and invention is to raise the 'rate of return over cost' and so enlarge the opportunities for investment. For example, he stated that:[21]

'The range of man's investment opportunity widens as his knowledge extends and his utilisation of the forces and materials of Nature grows. With each advance in knowledge come new opportunities to invest. The rate of return over cost rises'

and also that the rate of return over cost

'rises and falls according as the introduction or the exploitation of inventions is active or inactive.'[22]

In chapter 12 of The General Theory, Keynes considered in detail some of the factors which determine the prospective yield of an asset and hence its marginal efficiency:[23]

'The considerations upon which expectations of prospective yields are based are partly existing facts which we can assume to be known more or less for certain, and partly future events which can only be forecasted with more or less confidence. Amongst the first may be mentioned the existing stock of various types of capital-assets and of capital-assets in general and the strength of the existing consumers' demand for goods which require for their efficient production a relatively larger assistance from capital. Amongst the latter are future changes in the type and quantity of the stock of capital-assets and in the tastes of the consumer, the strength of effective demand from time to time during the life of the investment under consideration, and the changes in the wage-unit in terms of money which may occur during its life. We may sum up the state of psychological expectation which covers the latter as being the state of long-term expectation.'

20 Wicksell (1936), p. 134.
21 Fisher (1930), p. 341.
22 ibid., pp. 346–347.
23 Keynes (1936), pp. 147–148.

Keynes described long-term expectations as being formulated by taking the existing situation and projecting it into the future, modified only to the extent that we have more or less definite reasons for expecting a change:[24]

'The state of long-term expectation . . . depends on the confidence with which we make this forecast—on how highly we rate the likelihood of our best forecast turning out quite wrong . . . The state of confidence . . . is a matter to which practical men always pay the closest and most anxious attention . . . its relevance to economic problems comes in through its important influence on the marginal efficiency of capital.'

However, Keynes was forced to conclude that there is not much to be said *a priori* about the state of confidence:[25]

'Our conclusions (about the state of confidence) must mainly depend upon the actual observation of (stock) markets and business psychology.'

Hansen (1951) has noted that Keynes distinguished between '(a) a schedule of the marginal efficiency of capital "coolly considered" in terms of a realistic appraisal of capital requirements from the standpoint of long-term considerations of growth; and (b) a schedule of the marginal efficiency of capital, based on highly volatile and illusory expectations of yield-errors of optimism being rapidly replaced by errors of pessimism once doubt enters and begins to spread.[26] Hansen designated the former as the realistic schedule, and the latter as the volatile schedule.

Considering only the realistic schedule, various authors have made a careful, and often mathematically elegant, analysis of the factors determining the level of investment implied by the Keynesian formulation. For example, Klein has shown how it is 'possible to develop a definite relationship between the demand for capital goods and certain strategic economic variables':[27]

'The individual firm tries to maximise its expected profits subject to the constraint that it operates within the framework of certain technological conditions. The profits depend upon prices, sales, the use of factors of production and the costs of these factors. Furthermore the technological constraint established a definite relation between the input of the factors of production and the output of the final product. The maximisation of profit subject to the constraint leads immediately to Keynes' proposition that more capital goods will be demanded as long as their price is less than the discounted value of their expected future earnings.

24 ibid., pp. 148–149.
25 ibid., p. 149.
26 Hansen (1951), p. 338.
27 Klein (1966), pp. 62–63.

'The corresponding relation which holds for the economy as a whole, provided we have measured the aggregates properly, states that the community of entrepreneurs will demand more capital goods as long as their average price is less than the discounted value of their anticipated earning stream. There is a very elegant mathematical result . . . which shows that if the technological (input–output) relation for the economy as a whole follows certain very well established empirical forms then the equilibrium (profit-maximising) demand for capital goods depends upon the ratio of the discounted future national income to the average price of capital goods and upon the accumulated stock of capital. If we make the further assumptions that the expected national income depends upon the most recently observed levels of national income (how else can expectations be formed?) and that there is only one price level in the system, then we have the following fundamental Keynesian relationship:

'The demand for capital goods depends upon the real value of national income, the interest rate and the stock of accumulated capital.'

This approach has been criticised by Jorgenson who stresses the difference between the price of investment goods and the user cost of capital services[28]—a distinction which Klein admits to be valid. Jorgenson has himself developed a theory of investment on the basis of the neoclassical theory of optimal capital accumulation, with specific reference to the influence of United States tax policies on investment decisions.[29] He begins from the proposition that, 'reduced to its barest essentials, the neoclassical theory requires only that the criterion for optimal capital accumulation be the maximisation of utility of a stream of consumption. This basic assumption may be combined with any number of technological possibilities for production and economic possibilities for transformation of the results of production into a stream of consumption'.[30] He assumes that the set of technological possibilities may be described by a production function relating the flow of output to flows of labour services, capital services and materials. A firm is considered to supply capital services to itself through the acquisition of investment goods; the rate of change in the flow of capital services is proportional to the rate of acquisition of investment goods less the rate of replacement of previously acquired investment goods. It is further assumed that the results of the productive process may be transformed into a stream of consumption under a fixed set of prices for output, labour services, materials, investment goods, and consumption goods. Under these assumptions, the problem of maximising the utility of a consumption stream may be carried out in two stages; first, a production

28 A detailed discussion of the concept of user cost is provided by Lewis (1961), pp. 33–45.
29 See particularly Jorgenson (1965) and Jorgenson (1967).
30 Jorgenson (1967), p. 135.

plan may be chosen so as to maximise the present value of the productive enterprise; second, a consumption stream is chosen so as to maximise utility subject to the present value of the firm determined by production. The theory of investment results from a consideration of the problem of choosing a production plan which maximises the present value of the firm.

The present value of the firm is defined as the integral of discounted future revenues less discounted future outlays on both current and capital account, where outlays include direct taxes. This is to be maximised subject to two constraints. First, where K is the flow of capital services, L the flow of labour services, and Q the flow of output, levels of output and input are constrained by a production function.

$$F(Q, L, K) = 0 \qquad (2.2)$$

Secondly, the rate of change of the flow of capital services is proportional to the flow of net investment, with a constraint of proportionality of unity. Net investment is equal to total investment less replacement, where replacement is assumed to be proportional to capital stock.[31] Thus this constraint takes the form

$$\dot{K} = I - \delta K \qquad (2.3)$$

where $\dot{K}$ is the time rate of change of the flow of capital services, and δ is the rate of depreciation.

Jorgenson considered the United States corporate tax structure in which u is the rate of taxation of net income defined for tax purposes, and v, w and x are the proportions of depreciation, cost of capital and capital loss which may be charged against revenue less outlay on current account in measuring income for tax purposes. The Euler conditions for capital input and output necessary for the maximisation of the present value of the firm subject to these constraints yield the marginal productivity condition:

$$\frac{\delta Q}{\delta K} = \frac{q\left\{\left[\frac{1-uv}{1-u}\right]\delta + \left[\frac{1-uw}{1-u}\right]r - \left[\frac{1-ux}{1-u}\right]\frac{\dot{q}}{q}\right\}}{p} = \frac{c}{p} \qquad (2.4)$$

where p and q are the prices of output and investment in capital stock respectively, r is the cost of capital and $-\dot{q}/q$ the rate of capital loss.

31 This assumption is justified by a result of renewal theory which shows that, for a population of capital equipment, replacement investment approaches a constant proportion of capital stock, whatever the distribution of replacements for an individual member of the population, provided the size of the capital stock is constant or that the stock is growing at a constant rate. A proof of this theorem is given by Feller (1957), pp. 285–293.

The expression c may be interpreted as the implicit rental price for capital services supplied by the firm to itself—this is 'the user cost of capital'. User cost is then a shadow price which may be employed by the firm in the computation of an optimal path for accumulation of capital; to achieve this end the firm should charge itself a rental price for capital services equal to the user cost of capital at each point in time and should then continuously maximise profit in the usual way.

Within this framework, the level of output and the levels of all inputs, both current and capital, are determined from the production function and the marginal productivity conditions. If there is no lag in the completion of investment projects, the level of investment is determined from the constraint that the rate of change of capital stock is equal to investment less replacement. However, Jorgenson realistically assumes that time is required for the completion of investment projects, and replaces the assumption of equality between the actual and desired levels of capital stock by an equality between the level of capital stock which is desired and the level actually held plus the backlog of uncompleted investment projects for the expansion of capital stock. On the assumption that the level of output is determined by the Cobb–Douglas production function

$$Q = A K^a L^\beta \tag{2.5}$$

(where A, a and β are constants) and the marginal productivity condition for current output (given the actual level of capital stock), the desired capital stock K^* is given by

$$K^* = a \frac{pQ}{c} \tag{2.6}$$

The change in the desired capital stock resulting from a change in the rate of interest is given by

$$\frac{K^*}{r} = \frac{\left(a \dfrac{pQ}{c}\right)}{r}$$

$$= \frac{-a\,pQ}{c^2} \cdot q \cdot \frac{(1-uw)}{(1-u)} \tag{2.7}$$

Since p, Q, c and q are all positive and, under any feasible tax system, $(1-uw)$ and $(1-u)$ will be positive, it follows that the desired capital stock is inversely related to the rate of interest. The level of investment which, for any given change in the desired capital stock, depends on the rate at which the adjustment process proceeds, is consequently also inversely related to the rate of interest.

A similar methodological approach has been followed by Hammer (1964), who considered the behaviour necessary for a firm to achieve an optimal portfolio of its assets and liabilities; that is, one which maximises the profits resulting from its portfolio. The marginal yield on assets is taken as a non-increasing function of the stock of assets (an implication shown to result from horizontal or downward-sloping demand curves in the market in which the firm sells its output); and the cost of liabilities is taken as an increasing function of the firm's debt-equity ratio. Hammer claimed that this assumption, which is fundamental to his analysis, is reasonable and quoted in support Modigliani and Miller (1958) who argued that 'economic theory and market experience both suggest that the yields demanded by lenders tend to increase with the debt-equity ratio of the borrowing firm'.[32] The constraint within which portfolio adjustment decisions are assumed to be made is that the wealth of the firm is determined by the market value of the original portfolio. Subject to this constraint it is possible to derive an expression for the desired stock of assets, and then by assuming that investment is proportional to the difference between this desired stock and the firm's existing stock, an investment function can be obtained. When aggregated, and expressed in a form convenient for empirical investigation, Hammer found the investment function to be increasing with respect to wealth and expected yields, and decreasing with respect to interest rates and the existing capital stock.

The theoretical approaches to the study of investment behaviour discussed in this section have all reached the conclusion that investment is inversely related to the rate of interest. Moreover, as discussed by Gehrels and Wiggins (1957), the rate of interest tends to be indicative of the availability of credit, as well as directly measuring its cost. These authors supported their contention by describing the typical influence of central bank behaviour on the demand for loans and their supply by the commercial banking sector.[33]

'When the central bank pushes up the yields of short-term government securities, banks and non-bank lenders will increase the share of short-term government bonds in their portfolio at the expense of other earning assets. This action reduces reserves for the banking system as a whole and causes further restriction of loans to business borrowers. Conversely, when the central bank pushes down money-market rates, the decreased attractiveness of short-term yields, and the increase of reserves, will lead to increased availability of loans funds at relatively unchanging cost. In addition, it is some-

32 Modigliani and Miller (1958), p. 273. See also the discussions of this topic in ch. 2 § 5.
33 Gehrels and Wiggins (1957), p. 79.

times argued that banks and non-bank lenders consider probable movements of intermediate and long-term security prices. The fear of capital losses induced by a rising pattern of interest rates may cause prospective bond purchasers to hold off until they expect no further rise of rates. At the same time, potential borrowers who expect to need additional credit in the future may become fearful of not getting suitable accommodation at a future date, and in consequence restrict their present borrowing and expenditure commitments.'

Specific institutional characteristics, and particularly behavioural customs, may make the importance of central bank policy ever greater. This is illustrated by the role of the official re-discount rate (Bank Rate) in the United Kingdom money market as summarised by Kareken:[34]

'Among London clearing banks . . . there is little if any rate competition for . . . loans (advances) . . . They do not collude, but rather openly agree on what . . . rate to charge. When Bank rate is increased, clearing bank . . . loan rates are immediately increased; when decreased, these rates are immediately decreased. Marginal . . . borrowers presumably shift from market to market as relative interest rates change. The authorities should be thought of as being able, by increasing Bank rate, to increase nearly all market interest rates, or, at the very least, most short-term rates, and by decreasing Bank rate to decrease nearly all market rates. Clearly, changing Bank rate is not an empty gesture.'

Moreover, both the level of and changes in official re-discount rates, and hence other interest rates, tend to be associated with other forms of government influence on bank lending. In the United Kingdom these have taken the form of special requests to the commercial banks to limit their lending and the system of special deposits. The latter operates by requesting the banks to deposit a certain percentage of their total deposits with the central bank; this action reduces the banks' liquid assets to total deposits ratio, which they are then intended to restore by reducing loans. The system of special deposits has been extensively used in the United Kingdom in the 1960's, replacing the less formal system of special requests which was common in the mid-1950's. The system of special requests—'jawbone control'—has also been practised in the United States.

However, empirical investigations of both the questionnaire and econometric types have suggested that investment is relatively insensitive to the rate of interest. Whilst there may be valid grounds for questioning the conclusions drawn from these empirical investigations,[35] attention must also be directed towards a reconsideration of the assumptions underlying the neoclassical framework and the optimisation assumption in particular.

34 Kareken (1968), pp. 69–70.
35 See ch. 3 § 2 and ch. 4 § 1.

2.4. Criticisms of the Neoclassical Theories

The neoclassical theory of optimal capital accumulation as described by Fisher and developed by Jorgenson ignores the effects of uncertainty and risk. However, Keynes did state that explicit consideration should be given to risk when constructing the marginal efficiency of capital schedule. He discussed two types of risk: (i) the entrepreneur's risk that the anticipated yields may not actually be earned, and (ii) the lender's risk that the entrepreneur may default—this risk does not, of course, arise if the entrepreneur employs his own funds. Since the entrepreneur's forecast of the yields which will accrue from a proposed capital expenditure involves forecasts of both the sales receipts resulting from the use of the capital good and of the other costs associated with the productive process, neither of which can easily be forecast with accuracy, the first type of risk is likely to be very important. Keynes allowed for these risks by suggesting that a pure rate of return over cost comparable with a pure rate of interest could be obtained by discounting the series of expected annual returns after allowance for a risk insurance. Moreover, he argued that the entrepreneur's risk is 'susceptible to diminution by averaging as well as by increased accuracy of foresight'.[36] In this claim however, he seems to have overlooked the individuality and uniqueness which characterises many proposed investment projects. Firms often do not have the opportunity to average out the gains and losses which would be experienced if the act of investment could be repeated many times; neither is the experience of one project necessarily a relevant guide in any future situation. Faced with the problem of deciding whether or not to adopt any single investment opportunity, a firm is likely to pay particular attention to the least favourable possible outcomes, and to require a substantial reward over the expected rate of return for undertaking the risk. Duesenberry (1958) quoted an example to show how this attitude may substantially reduce the sensitivity of investment to the rate of interest:[37]

'Suppose a firm requires that an investment have an expected yield of 10% after taxes and interest charges before it can be undertaken. If the tax rate on income is 50% and the interest rate 2%, the expected yield before interest and taxes must be 22%. If the interest rate is 4%, the required yield before taxes and interest rises to 24%. A 100% increase in the interest rate raises the required return by only 9%. Even if the elasticity of the marginal efficiency schedule (in terms of expected returns before taxes) were substantial, investment would appear to be inelastic to the interest rate.'

36 Keynes (1936), p. 144.
37 Duesenberry (1958), p. 50.

Risk and uncertainty increase the further one looks into the future, and Shackle (1946) has shown how entrepreneurial recognition of this factor can further reduce the influence of the rate of interest on investment:[38]

'The strength of the influence of interest-rates on the pace of investment in those kinds of equipment which are subject to the hazards of invention and fashion can be rendered negligible by an allowance, of a size such as enterprisers themselves imply that they adopt,[39] for doubt concerning the correctness of the "best guess" they can make, on available knowledge, as to the size of future net returns from such equipment; provided the form of this allowance is that of a rate used for discounting in the same manner as the interest-rate, or is some other strongly-increasing function of futurity.'

The neoclassical theory of capital accumulation also assumes that firms operate in a perfect capital market, so that the marginal cost to a firm of raising capital is simply the market rate of interest. Hence, following Keynes' formulation, since the level of investment is determined by the intersection of the marginal efficiency of capital and the marginal cost of capital schedules, it follows that the quantitative effect of changes in the rate of interest is determined by the elasticity of the marginal efficiency of capital schedule. Hansen (1951) has claimed that 'in industrially advanced countries . . . the investment demand schedule . . . tends to be fairly interest-inelastic'.[40] If this claim—whose validity can only be assessed empirically—is correct, variations in the rate of interest will have only little effect on investment.

A more fundamental criticism concerns an assumption implicit in all formulations of the neoclassical theories, namely that firms operate as knowledgeable and efficient profit maximisers. Given the difficulties involved in forecasting the marginal efficiency of a proposed capital project, the question arises of whether or not firms actually perform the necessary calculations; and, if they do not, what the consequences are for the validity of theories of investment developed around such calculations? The rule that an investment will be profitable if its marginal efficiency exceeds the rate of interest is a rule of rational behaviour; but are firms rational? Ackley (1961) reported that:[41]

'The opinions of well-informed observers, plus some scanty evidence from surveys, indicate that investment decisions are often based on hunch or whim or prejudice, on noneconomic factors, or, where calculations are made, on rules of thumb that occasionally cause the selection of unprofitable alternatives or, more frequently, rejection of profitable investments.'

38 Shackle (1946), p. 16.
39 See, for example, Andrews (1940).
40 Hansen (1951), p. 135.
41 Ackley (1961), p. 476.

Recent examples of evidence relating to the British economy which are consistent with Ackley's statement are provided by Barna (1962), N.E.D.C. (1965) and Williams and Scott (1965).

More fundamentally, the assumption that firms aim to maximise their profits has been disputed by many observers of the modern business scene. There are two main criticisms of the assumption. Firstly, although it may be true that entrepreneurs are efficient utility maximisers, it does not follow that they are profit maximisers. Profits may be only one of several objectives sought by entrepreneurs; other objectives may be power, prestige, a desire to own a large firm, and a sense of satisfaction from fulfilling public needs. Moreover, many entrepreneurs desire leisure; as Hicks said, 'the best of all monopoly profits is a quiet life'.[42] Recognition of this fact of life has led to the concept of 'satisficing'; that is, a form of behaviour in which the subject, faced with a difficult problem to solve, prefers to sacrifice some of the rewards of the optimum solution in order to reduce the pains incurred in searching for it.[43] Secondly, the structure of a modern company involves a division of the entrepreneurial roles of ownership and management such that these roles are played by different groups of persons who may have conflicting interests. In particular, the diffusion of ownership through the multiplicity of the number of shareholders combined with the increasingly technical nature of large-scale organisation has increased the power of management vis-a-vis that of the shareholders. Marris (1964), after considering the psychological, sociological and economic influences on managers, came to the conclusion that these pressures 'lead managers to maximise the rate of growth of the firm they are employed in, subject to a constraint imposed by the security motive'.[44] This objective is essentially similar to the commonly-accepted one of maximising the money value of sales subject to a constraint that profits do not fall below some acceptable minimum level.

2.5. Sources of Funds

One particular assumption of the conventional neoclassical theories—that firms operate in a perfect capital market—has received wide criticism. In such a capital market, the rational entrepreneur should have no preference for using his own rather than borrowed funds because, by definition, the opportunity cost of using internally-generated funds is equal to the cost of obtaining external funds. However, obser-

---

42 Hicks (1935), p. 8.
43 On this subject, see Simon (1957, 1959).
44 Marris (1964), p. 47.

vation of the behaviour of modern companies has led to the conclusion that their managers have a definite preference for internal funds. For them, the imputed costs of using internal funds must be less than the costs (both direct monetary and subjective) of obtaining external funds. The construction of a marginal cost of funds schedule which recognises this feature of investment financing has been tackled by Hoover (1954), Duesenberry (1958) and Merrett and Sykes (1963).

A firm is able to obtain funds for investment from several different sources, of which the most important are: (i) its depreciation allowances; (ii) its net profits, where net profits = after-tax profits – depreciation allowances; (iii) various types of fixed interest borrowing; (iv) preference shares; (v) equity issues.

When a firm uses its own profits, part of the total (monetary and subjective) cost involved is the opportunity cost of not using the funds for other purposes. Thus the opportunity cost is the return which the firm could obtain by buying government bonds or the shares of other companies, or the saving in interest payments which it would realise by repaying any existing debt of its own. These opportunity costs are likely to be related to the yield offered by a safe financial investment. Hoover has argued that the subjective costs to a firm of using its depreciation allowances are less than those associated with using its other profits since 'firms frequently report that they regard depreciation funds as quasi-automatically earmarked for investment and as constituting a sort of basic minimum (level of investment)'.[45] Duesenberry, and Merrett and Sykes, on the other hand, did not make this distinction, but claimed that a subjective cost arises if the firm retains such a large proportion of its profits that its dividend pay-out ratio falls below that considered 'normal' by its shareholders and the stock market. They argued that the share price would fall, thus perhaps permanently depressing its long-term level, and raising the long-term cost of borrowing. This assertion is supported by empirical studies: Lintner (1956) found that U.S. managements are very reluctant to reduce their dividend rate; and Prais (1959), after a study of the published accounts of a sample of U.K. firms, concluded that distribution policy has been relatively stable.

Borrowing takes the form of bank overdrafts, and medium and long-term loans. Bank overdrafts are the most flexible form of borrowing in that the borrower has the right to repay the overdraft in whole or in part at any time. However, the bank may have a similar right to require repayment at any time; thus firms typically use bank overdrafts to finance 'working capital'. In comparison, most medium and long-term

45 Hoover (1954), p. 205.

loans are repayable only at a specified future date, and because of this sometimes command a higher interest rate. Borrowing also involves some subjective costs. Besides the aversion which most firms have to borrowing, and to its associated risks, the fixed interest charges increase the effect of fluctuations in demand on the after-tax profits out of which firms pay their dividends, thus perhaps necessitating a dividend reduction. Partly for this reason, and partly because the risk premium required by a lender will increase as the amount borrowed increases, the total costs of borrowing are likely to be dependent upon the ratio of the firm's debt to its earnings.

Preference shares are in some respects similar to long-term loans, but as they carry title to part ownership of the firm, they receive their return only when other lenders have received their full interest payment. Because of this greater risk, they usually bear a higher rate of interest than long-term loans.

Equity issues take one of two forms: new issues and rights issues. New issues of equity capital are primarily used by 'relatively recently established companies whose capital needs have outgrown the resources available from existing shareholders or by private companies converting to public companies'.[46] The immediate costs of new issues are the issue and administrative expenses, including advertising, plus the cost of any discount at which the new issue is offered. Unfortunately, in order to evaluate the full cost of equity finance it is necessary to adopt a particular view about modern company organisation and motivation. A company's managers could argue that, besides the immediate direct expenses, the only costs incurred are those resulting from the obligation to pay subsequent dividends to the new shareholders. However, from the viewpoint of existing shareholders, new issues represent a dilution of their claim to ownership of the firm and a reduction of their possible capital growth prospects. Unfortunately this loss, being subject to so much uncertainty, is not easily measured. Rights issues have lower administrative expenses than new issues; this is partly because they usually require less advertising and partly because they need not involve any substantial underwriting commission. Moreover they have an imputed advantage in that, providing existing shareholders take up a higher proportion of rights issues than new issues, they should result in the aggregate value of the shares being slightly higher than after a new issue. (This assumes that existing shareholders value their shares at least marginally higher than non-shareholders.) In general, as Durand (1952) found, firms are generally concerned about their earnings record

46 Merrett and Sykes (1965), p. 82.

on a per-share basis, and are unwilling to finance investment by equity issues unless they can expect an improvement in their per-share earnings. Comparing the cost of equity finance with that of borrowing, Duesenberry stated that the cost of the former 'is substantially above the opportunity cost of using internally generated funds or small amounts of debt',[47] but that 'once returns are high enough to justify issuing equities, the cost-of-funds schedule becomes more elastic to the rate of return than in the range in which there is a large volume of debt outstanding but equities are not being sold'.[48]

These considerations can be presented in terms of a simple cost of funds schedule, as shown in fig. 2.1. In the construction of the schedule, it has been assumed that firms do not differentiate between their depreciation allowances and their 'normal' retention of net profits. Neither is a distinction drawn between the different types of external financing because, as Hoover pointed out, the choice between them varies so much according to the particular situation of each firm.

Tax considerations can also affect the relative costs of different sources of finance. For example, a tax system such as those of the United Kingdom and the United States which differentiates between distributed and undistributed profits, and which charges a higher rate on the former, will reduce the relative cost of using retained profits vis-a-vis equity issues.[49]

Replacing the assumption of a perfectly inelastic cost-of-funds schedule by one which recognises the relationship between the marginal cost of funds and the amount of funds required, complicates the theory of investment. Following the Keynesian approach, the rate of investment will be determined by the intersection of the marginal efficiency of capital and marginal cost-of-funds schedules. Since the schedules for many firms will intersect beyond the horizontal section of the cost-of-funds schedule, it would appear that the level of profits (either total after-tax or net of 'normal' dividend payments) is a major determinant of investment. As Lintner has shown most firms have some concept of a normal ratio of dividends to profits, which they adhere to fairly closely in practice. Thus, the distinction between these two definitions of profits may not be significant (statistically so, in empirical studies).

The theoretical case for arguing that profits, representing a source of funds, are a major determinant of aggregate investment expenditures has been questioned by Eisner and Strotz. It is only in an imperfect capital

47 Duesenberry (1958), p. 95.
48 ibid., p. 96.
49 For a discussion of the costs of alternative sources of capital which incorporates the effects of existing U.K. tax legislation, see Merrett and Sykes (1966), pp. 30–48.

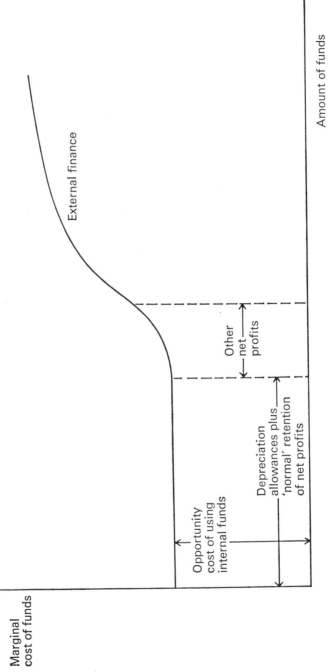

Fig. 2.1. Marginal Cost of Funds Schedule

market that the rate of profits enters into the cost-of-funds schedule, yet they claimed that even in such a market the role of profits might be primarily to determine which firms are able to invest, rather than aggregate investment. An increase in aggregate profits, other things being equal, will switch the distribution of income from wage-and-salary earners towards shareholders (distributed profits) and firms themselves (retained profits). Whilst this will increase the available supply of funds, it will also lower the average prosperity to consume, which in turn is likely to depress the marginal efficiency of capital schedule. Eisner and Strotz commented that:[50]

'without the assumption of perpetual full employment, it would seem difficult to argue with any assurance that lowering the propensity to consume (by altering the income distribution in favour of profits) would have a greater positive effect on investment as a consequence of lower interest rates (or easier supply of capital) than its negative effect as a consequence of the reduction in consumption demand.'

Unfortunately because of the widely observed correlation between profits and sales (or output) this proposition is not readily amenable to statistical verification. Fluctuations in aggregate profits are more the result of cyclical swings and general economic growth than of changes in the distribution of income.

Taken together, the criticisms of the neoclassical theory presented in this and the previous section suggest that the rate of interest might be of less importance and the flow of profits of more importance than that theory predicts. The next section discusses an alternative and important theory of investment not explicitly based on any optimising assumptions.

2.6. The Acceleration Principle

The genesis of the acceleration principle is often linked with the name of J. M. Clark who in 1917 analysed its fundamental features. These are that 'the demand for enlarging the means of production . . . varies, not with the demand for the finished product, but rather with the acceleration of that demand';[51] and that 'the total demand for producers' goods tends to vary more sharply than the demand for finished products'.[52] However, these ideas had been presented several years earlier by Aftalion (1909) who as an illustrative example considered the following purely hypothetical case'.[53]

50 Eisner and Strotz (1963), pp. 124–125. See also Lange (1938).
51 Clark (1917), p. 234.
52 ibid., p. 235.
53 Reproduced from Hansen (1951), p. 357.

'An industry requires a hundred thousand looms. The average length of life of these looms is ten years. Then ten thousand looms are to be replaced each year. If, now, the consumers' demand increases 10 per cent, there is an additional need for ten thousand new looms. Thus a 10 per cent increase in consumer demand gives rise to a 100 per cent increase in the demand for fixed capital.

The formal algebraic statement of the acceleration principle rests on a number of rigid assumptions; however, these may be partially reduced without affecting the essence of the principle.[54] The assumptions are that:

(i) at every moment of time, and for every level of production, there is an invariant optimum method of production. Firms combine capital and labour in exactly the same proportions, irrespective of the prevailing levels of wage rates and interest rates, and hence they have fixed optimum capital/output and labour/output ratios.

(ii) the proportions in which different types of products are produced are similarly invariant.

(iii) firms are not deterred from expanding their capital equipment by any shortage of available funds.

(iv) in each time period, a firm undertakes sufficient investment to equate its capital stock with that which is optimum for the current level of production.

(v) net investment is not undertaken for any other purposes.

Hence, at the end of each period, the existing capital stock is equal to the optimum capital stock. Denoting the capital stock at the end of each period by $\bar{K}$, the output of each period by Y, the optimum capital/output ratio by β and using the time subscript t to denote the period, the assumptions imply that

$$\bar{K}_{t-1} = \beta Y_{t-1}, \tag{2.8}$$

and

$$\bar{K}_t = \beta Y_t, \tag{2.9}$$

Subtracting equation (2.9) from equation (2.8) gives

$$\bar{K}_t - \bar{K}_{t-1} = \beta(Y_t - Y_{t-1}) \tag{2.10}$$

54 This was recognised by Clark who wrote: 'The law may be expressed algebraically, if the reader remembers that it only represents a mechanical view of the situation, and supplies for himself an allowance for elements not included in the formula'. Clark (1917), p. 222.

The difference between $\bar{K}_{t-1}$ and $\bar{K}_t$ is the net investment in period t, and so equation (2.10) states that net investment is a function of the rate of change of output. This rigid formulation of the acceleration principle has been attacked by many authors, but probably the most complete statements of its defects have been made by Tinbergen (1938) and Knox (1952). Tinbergen, particularly, was critical of the assumptions on which the principle is based. Referring to assumption (i), he pointed out that 'the acceleration principle can only be true . . . if . . . (there are) . . . no abrupt changes in technique leading to a sudden increase in the amount of capital goods necessary to the production of one unit of consumers' goods'.[55] In contradiction to assumption (iii), he consistently argued that profits are an important determinant of investment.

An important and necessary condition for the acceleration principle is that firms operate at a fixed level of capacity utilisation; this follows from the constraint that firms must maintain a constant relationship between their capital stock and their output, which in turn is implied by assumptions (i), (iv) and (v). Further, many authors argue that this level must be that of full capacity utilisation, since as Clark recognised:[56]

'. . . the first increase in demand for finished products can be taken care of by utilising the excess producing capacity which an industry using much machinery habitually carries over a period of depression.'

As industries are frequently observed to have excess capacity in a depression, the rigid acceleration principle thus involves a very unrealistic assumption. Moreover, as Tinbergen argued, the accelerator mechanism is likely to be asymmetrical between the upswing and downswing stages of the economic cycle:[57]

'Very strong decreases in consumers' goods production must not occur. If the principle were right, they would lead to a corresponding disinvestment and this can only take place to the extent of replacement. If annual replacement amounts to 10 per cent of the stock of capital goods, then a larger decrease in this stock than 10 per cent per annum is impossible. A decrease in consumers' goods production of 15 per cent could not lead to a 15 per cent decrease in physical capital as the acceleration principle would require. It is interesting that this limit is sharper the greater the duration of life of the capital goods considered.'

Tinbergen's criticism assumes that firms do not scrap their capital stock (beyond that required by normal replacement) during a depression, but

55 Tinbergen (1938), pp. 165–166.
56 Clark (1917), p. 226.
57 Tinbergen (1938), p. 165.

since this assumption is realistic, the criticism is generally accepted. Tinbergen continued his argument to stress that it is only when production has reached full capacity that 'the necessity of the principles' action recurs'.[58]

This latter criticism raises two important problems. Firstly, if the economy is working at full capacity, how is it possible for an increase in production to occur without the assistance of the corresponding increase in the capital stock, which the acceleration principle is itself supposed to induce? Although the simplest form of the acceleration principle, in which the increase in production and the net investment occur simultaneously, is often modified to allow for gestation lags in the production of the capital goods, in no formulation does the net investment precede the increase in production. An escape from this dilemma was provided by Staehle who suggested that the relationship be between net investment and the shift in the demand curve for consumers' goods instead of the increase in the actual quantity demanded or produced.[59] As Tinbergen pointed out, Staehle's hypothesis can be given an especially convenient form if the elasticity of demand is unity (which, approximately, will be the case for 'all consumption'): then the shift in demand curve is simply equal to the change in money value of consumption or consumption outlay.

The second problem arises from the difficulty of defining a meaningful and measurable concept of capacity. Knox considered four possible alternative definitions in terms of a single firm:

(i)   the point at which its average total cost curve becomes vertical.
(ii) 'practical' capacity; i.e., the output that a firm can maintain for a reasonable period with a given plant, making due allowance for such factors as seasonal fluctuations, repairs, obsolescence, and customs and regulations governing hours of work.
(iii) the output at a firm's minimum average total cost.
(iv) where marginal cost equals marginal revenue.

The first definition is clearly too rigid—it is unlikely that full capacity in this sense is ever attained. The second, whilst more realistic, is too imprecise to be of practical value. The fourth suffers from the defect that it is not independent of the demand situation; moreover, so far as firms seek to maximise profits they will always be operating at full capacity according to this definition. Knox concluded that the third definition is the most satisfactory, and on the basis of it, attributed a rational basis to the acceleration principle:[60]

58 ibid., p. 166.
59 See ibid., p. 168.
60 Knox (1952), p. 279.

'it may be interpreted to mean that entrepreneurs will meet a rise in demand by expanding their plant, where the cost of producing the extra output with the existing plant exceeds the operating cost with the enlarged plant plus the costs of purchasing and installing it. If we assume with the acceleration principle that changes in output are the only forces making for investment, we may conclude that there is no incentive for investment before the least cost point is reached, and an increasing incentive the further beyond that point output goes.'

Other authors have also sought to attribute a rational profit-maximising basis to the acceleration principle. For example, Eisner (1960) identified his particular version of the acceleration principle with:[61]

'a world of risk and uncertainty in which business firms strive to maximise the mathematical expectation of some monotonic increasing function of expected future profit, subject to a production function with decreasing marginal returns to each factor and positive cross partial derivatives. This means, in particular, that for a firm initially in equilibrium it pays to increase the stock of capital for permanent or certainly expected increases in demand for output.'

Like the neoclassical theory of capital accumulation, the acceleration principle has been criticised for its lack of precision about the timing of investment. Following the argument of Knox outlined above, 'from the moment at which least cost output is passed there is a possibility of investment; but there is no knowing just when the decision to invest will be taken'.[62] Strictly speaking however, for assumption (iv) to hold, the full adjustment must take place within one unit period. The restrictiveness of this assumption is further illustrated by other problems relating to the timing of investment. Capital equipment tends to be obtainable and effective only in large units, and a small increase in production may not justify the purchase of even one additional unit. Long (1940) cited an example:[63]

'paper-making machines for the manufacture of newsprint paper come only in million dollar units capable of producing one-fourth the requirements of a good-sized plant and characterised by great durability.'

Even if the capital equipment is easily divisible, the process of installation may so hinder the current productive processes, that firms may wait until a large purchase is justified. Evidence of this phenomena was cited by Hultgren (1948):[64]

'no one railroad typically buys cars in continuous driblets; or at any rate small repetitive purchases can hardly account for any large part of total orders.'

61 Eisner (1960), p. 1.
62 ibid., p. 279.
63 Long (1940), pp. 61–62.
64 Hultgren (1948), p. 167.

On the other hand, although investment in a single productive process may be a discontinuous process, it is possible that aggregation to the successive levels of the firm, industry and whole economy may remove this difficulty.

This extensive criticism of the acceleration principle has not led to its total abandonment but to its gradual modification into the types of capital stock adjustment model described in ch. 2 § 9.

2.7 Replacement Investment

The acceleration principle relates to net investment and, without a complementary theory of replacement investment, it cannot provide an adequate theory of gross investment. A separate theory of replacement investment can only be developed if it is possible both to define and identify replacement as distinct from net investment. Hayek considered an act of investment as net only if the resulting stock of capital is expected to yield its owner an income stream greater than that which would otherwise have occurred.[65] This economic definition is of limited value since it is applicable only if forecasts of the future income stream to accrue from both the original and the resulting capital stocks can be made with certainty. A technological distinction is not usually of greater assistance since replacement is seldom made without improvement, and the net and replacement components of most investments cannot be clearly distinguished. However, such problems of definition and identification need not be a deterrent to the construction of a theory of replacement investment if the ultimate objective is simply to derive a theory of gross investment. When considering gross investment, errors of distinction between its net and replacement components will be of little importance, since they cancel out with each other.

The need for a separate theory of replacement investment may also be questioned—do not firms subject proposals for 'replacement' capital expenditure projects to exactly the same criteria as those used for 'expansion' projects? The Keynesian investment criteria of evaluating a project by comparing its marginal efficiency with the rate of interest can be expressed in a form different from that presented in ch. 2 § 3. The value of a capital good, V, is equal to the sum of the series of expected annual returns $(R_1, R_2, \ldots R_n)$ discounted back to the present at the current rate of interest, i. Thus

$$V = \frac{R_1}{1+i} + \frac{R_2}{(1+i)^2} + \ldots + \frac{R_n}{(1+i)^n} \qquad (2.11)$$

65 See Hayek (1941), pp. 300–301.

If C is the cost of the capital good, it will pay to purchase it so long as $V > C$. This criteria is in a form easily applicable to replacement problems. For example, consider one in which a firm is contemplating whether or not to replace an old with a new machine. For replacement to be profitable it is necessary for the discounted value of the expected annual returns from the new machine minus that from the old to exceed the cost of the new machine minus the scrap value of the old. As a theory of replacement this criteria is, however, subject to the same criticisms as those made of the theory of optimal capital accumulation, as outlined in ch. 2 § 4. Moreover, there is some evidence that firms consider replacement as more or less automatic. Barna, on the basis of a study of 35 U.K. firms, reported that different types of investment projects (e.g., replacement, expansion, cost-saving, etc.) are often subject to different standards of assessment: that it is usually easier to obtain approval for replacement schemes than for other projects; and that there may often be no profitability calculation for replacement investment. On the other hand, as Neild (1964) pointed out:[66]

'a replacement decision is a simpler decision surrounded by fewer uncertainties than a major expansion, or a venture into a new market. Compared with a major new investment, there is likely to be less uncertainty on the demand side; the calculations of costs with the new and old machine can be made with moderate accuracy and the cost of the new machine (unlike the costs of some large projects) is known fairly precisely in advance. In various respects, there is therefore greater scope for calculation when making a replacement decision than a new investment decision.'

Clark (1917) postulated that 'the demand for maintenance and replacement of existing capital varies with the amount of the demand for finished products'.[67] Since assumption (i) of the acceleration principle implies a fixed capital/output ratio, it follows that replacement investment must be a function of the size of the existing capital stock. Although this simple theory has been subjected to criticism, it has recently returned to favour. It implies that a constant proportion of the capital stock is replaced each year, irrespective of the age of the existing equipment and the current economic conditions. A simple, and seemingly more realistic, assumption is that each item of capital equipment is replaced at the end of its fixed lifetime, all items having the same lifetime. Thus replacement of each asset in each year is equal to gross investment, lagged by a number of years equal to the lifetime of the equipment. This modified theory has been subjected to further qualifica-

66 op. cit., p. 32.
67 Clark (1917), p. 220.

tions. Somers (1949) pointed out that replacement demand depends partly on the 'extent to which capital goods are used to produce "finished" products (in so far as depreciation is a function of use, i.e., through wear and tear or direct use in the process of production)'.[68] Kuznets has shown that, for machines with a constant rate of obsolescence, it pays to replace earlier at a higher level of output than at a lower.[69] However, this factor is not likely to be of great importance, as Kuznets himself recognised when he stated that the level of output will influence the replacement of only those items of equipment which are 'sufficiently near the end of their average period of life to be affected by the change in the prospective savings from the installation of new units'.[70] Tinbergen and Polak added further realism to the theory of replacement by pointing out that capital goods do not all have the same lifetimes, and that even a single item of capital equipment does not have a precise lifetime.[71] As shown by these latter authors these qualifications have the effect of dampening the replacement cycles likely to be generated by previous fluctuations in gross investment. Indeed, modern replacement theory confirms Clark's hypothesis that replacement investment varies with the size of the existing capital stock. Jorgenson reports that:[72]

'replacement . . . is a recurrent event. An initial increase in capacity generates replacements distributed over time; but each replacement generates a new set of replacements. This process repeats itself indefinitely. The appropriate model for replacement investment is not the distribution over time of the replacements for a single investment but rather the distribution over time of the infinite stream of replacements generated by a single investment. It is a fundamental result of renewal theory that the distribution of replacements for such an infinite stream approaches a constant fraction of capital stock for (almost) any distribution of replacements over time and for any initial age distribution of capital stock. This result holds for a constant stock and for a growing stock as well.'

The theory that replacement investment is a simple function of the existing capital stock has been incorporated in several theories of gross investment. Whereas the statistical examination of the theories which imply 'echo' effects require data on investment in each asset over a considerable number of years, this theory requires data on only the total existing capital stock. Its simplicity makes it very convenient for inclusion in econometric models of aggregate investment.

68 Somers (1949), p. 14.
69 See Kuznets (1935), pp. 238–243.
70 ibid., p. 241.
71 See Tinbergen and Polak (1950), pp. 178–180.
72 Jorgenson (1965), p. 51.

2.8. Expectations about the Future

The essence of any investment decision is that it is taken with regard to the future, rather than the current or past situation. As the future is unknown, only current expectations about what it holds can be incorporated into any theory of investment behaviour. Moreover, the expectations must be those of the decision-makers, not the theorist!

Four alternative types of assumptions about the future expectations of those responsible for investment decisions may be distinguished. Firstly, some theories incorporate the assumption that decision-makers act as if the current situation will not change. For example, the rigid acceleration principle implicitly assumes that the rate of output will continue as at present. Although this assumption has the important virtue of simplicity, it is usually unrealistic. If anything is certain in economics, it is that things will change, and decision-makers are presumably well aware of this fact. Moreover, the assumption of 'no change' rarely constitutes even an unbiased estimate of the likely outcome. Although economic phenomena are subject to irregular fluctuations, they often follow some general path. Output, consumption and prices are usually more likely to rise than fall. An obvious alternative is therefore to assume that decision-makers expect the relevant variables to change at a fixed and pre-specified rate. For example, de Leeuw (1962) in the construction of his theory of investment in the United States assumed that firms expect output to grow at a steady annual rate of 4%. However, although this growth rate was the average over the period de Leeuw was examining, it seems more likely that firms' views about future growth at any particular time are influenced by their recent experience. A common assumption is therefore that firms' expectations are determined by some particular spectrum of their previous experiences. As the subjective influence of such experiences is likely to diminish the more distant they are, the overall effect of the different past experiences has often been described by the geometrically declining lag distribution. Thus the expected value of a variable X in period t, denoted by $X_t{}^*$, is given by

$$X_t{}^* = (1-\lambda)\ X_t + (1-\lambda)\ \lambda\ X_{t-1} + (1-\lambda)\ \lambda^2\ X_{t-2} + \ldots$$

$$(2.12)$$

Although the problems encountered in incorporating such a theory of expectations into an econometric model of investment behaviour are discussed in ch. 4 § 2, 3, some points can be noted at this stage. Firstly, this theory of expectations implies that the expected value of a variable whose value has been increasing (decreasing) recently will be less (higher) than the most recent values. Thus it implies a turning point.

Secondly, like the other theories of expectations described above, it takes no account of the current levels of or recent changes in variables other than the one to which it explicitly relates.

Various authors have argued that particular economic variables capture or reflect the future expectations upon which investment decisions are based. For example, it has often been claimed that profits are an important determinant of investment not only because they are a source of funds but because they determine current expectations about the future. Tinbergen and Polak[73] wrote:

'To a very large extent, profit expectations will be based on current facts, in particular on the actual magnitude of profits . . . There is always a strong and well-understandable tendency to extrapolate the recent past and current events into the future.'

However, Eisner and Strotz discounted this argument by distinguishing between the profits earned on existing capital and the expected profits from new capital investment:[74]

'One should not expect a firm, no matter how high its current profits or expected future profits, to wish to invest unless the contemplated addition to capital stock is expected to increase expected profits, or have an expected return higher than that from alternative uses of funds.'

An alternative indication of expectations about future profitability is provided by the stock market valuation of firms since, in theory at least, the total value of a firm's shares is determined by the discounted value of its future earnings. The use of stock market indices to reflect changing business expectations is subject to two main criticisms. The first is that share price movements reflect the expectations of the stock market and not of the businessmen who actually take investment decisions. This criticism can be rejected if either of the following two propositions advanced by Meyer and Kuh (1957) can be accepted: (i) that both the stock market and individual firms observe the same information and react similarly in the formation of their expectations; (ii) that individual firms observe stock market behaviour and take it into account when making their investment plans. The first proposition can be accepted in so far as stock market fluctuations are due to correct calculation and reporting of firms' future prospects. Empirical support for the validity of the second has been provided by Barna (1962), who, after studying U.K. manufacturing industry firms reported:[75]

73 Tinbergen and Polak (1950), pp. 166–167.
74 Eisner and Strotz (1963), p. 124.
75 Barna (1962), p. 51.

'Businessmen . . . appear to be very much affected by daily events, including movements on the stock exchanges, but the effect is on their feeling of
confidence and not necessarily on their explicit assessment of the future.'

The second criticism of the use of share prices as an indicator of
business expectations is that they are too volatile and too responsive to
the day-to-day political and economic events which probably have little
influence on long-run business profitability. This criticism runs counter
both to Keynes' view of the volatility of business expectations and to the
finding of Barna just quoted. Moreover, the day-to-day fluctuations can
be removed by averaging the market indices over, say, successive quarterly periods. Finally, even if share price indices exaggerate the movements in 'rational' business expectations, they may nevertheless be
perfectly correlated with them. Thus, whilst no one is likely to claim
that stock market indices are the best possible measure of the relevant
business expectations, they are probably one of the best of those that
are easily and widely available.

Other possible indications of business expectations are provided by
so-called leading indicators and regular questionnaire surveys of
business behaviour. Examples of leading business cycle indicators which
have been used to reflect expectations are the ratio of new orders to
capacity[76] and the change in unfilled orders.[77] Some of the regular
questionnaire studies of business prospects and behaviour, now conducted in several countries, include direct questions about future expectations. For example, the four-monthly industrial trends survey conducted by the Confederation of British Industry asks firms if they are
more, or less, optimistic than they were four months ago about the
general business situation in their industry. Answers are reported in
the form of the percentage of firms replying 'more', 'same', or 'less',
and by cumulating the balance of these replies over time a continuing
index of business expectations may be obtained.

2.9. Capital Stock Adjustment Models

The development of capital stock adjustment models can be traced
back to Goodwin (1948, 1951). Criticising the acceleration principle
for its assumption that capital is always perfectly adjusted to output,
he suggested that 'the rate of investment is proportional to the difference
between the equilibrium or ideal quantity of capital, and the actual
quantity',[78] the former being 'given by the real national output and the

76 See, for example, Hart (1965).
77 See, for example, Eckstein (1965).
78 Goodwin (1948), p. 120.

state of technology'.[79] Like Hicks (1950), Goodwin considered both the distributed lag effects of output on investment, and the ceiling to investment which results from the capacity of the capital goods industries and/or full employment.

The models constructed by these two authors represented crucial elements in their general analysis of business-cycle fluctuations. A specific theory of net investment, developed in a form amenable to econometric investigation, was subsequently presented by Chenery (1952). This theory took account of both the existence and the desirability (up to a certain limit) of excess capacity. Starting from the rigid accelerator as specified in (2.10),

$$\bar{K}_t - \bar{K}_{t-1} = \beta\,(Y_t - Y_{t-1}),$$

Chenery first assumed that entrepreneurs' reaction to an initial change in output would be neither instantaneous nor complete, and so reformulated the hypothesis as

$$\Delta\bar{K}_{t+\theta} = \bar{K}_{t+\theta} - \bar{K}_{t+\theta-1} = \beta\delta(Y_t - Y_{t-1}) \qquad (2.13)$$

where θ is the time lag between an output change and the corresponding induced investment, and δ is a reaction coefficient. The time lag is introduced partly to cover the gestation period of the required capital goods but also 'because entrepreneurs take past as well as current changes in output as an indication of demand'.[80] The reaction coefficient is introduced to make some allowance for the effects of over-capacity since in this situation, 'we can assume that the investment induced by a given change in demand will be less than the amount required to provide an equal amount of new capacity'.[81] But the introduction of a reaction coefficient still leaves the acceleration principle in an unrealistic form, for, as Chenery noted:[82]

'(It) does not allow for the chief discrepancy between the simple accelerator assumption and observed behaviour; the fact that capital is not and cannot be contracted as rapidly as it expands. Unless we limit the acceleration principle to periods of full utilisation of capacity, it will forecast too rapid a decrease of capacity in a downswing and too rapid an increase in recovery.'

Chenery attempted to overcome this problem by replacing the assumption that net investment is proportional to the change in output by an assumption that it is proportional to the deviation of actual

79 Goodwin (1951), p. 438.
80 Chenery (1952), p. 12.
81 ibid., p. 12.
82 ibid., p. 12.

output from 'normal' output. Normal output is specified with reference to the existing capital stock; in period t it is $\bar{K}_t/\beta$. The reformulation gives

$$\Delta \bar{K}_{t+\theta} = \delta(\beta Y_t - \bar{K}_t) \qquad (2.14)$$

Chenery labelled the behaviour implied by equation (2.14) as a 'pursuit curve', since 'entrepreneurs are trying to balance capacity against output but do not invest (or disinvest) the whole amount necessary to do so in any one period'.[83]

In an earlier section of his paper, Chenery had shown that 'if firms seek to minimise the cost of production over time, and if there are economies of scale, they will tend to build ahead of demand and will have a normal degree of overcapacity. Equation (2.14) was thus further modified so that net investment became proportional to the difference between the amount of capital needed to produce the current output (βY_t) and the optimum utilisation of the existing capital stock ($\lambda \bar{K}_t$), where λ is the optimum rate of capacity utilisation. Thus

$$\Delta \bar{K}_{t+\theta} = \delta(\beta Y_t - \lambda \bar{K}_t) \qquad (2.15)$$

However, even in this formulation, the value of δ is likely to depend on whether or not current output is greater or less than normal output. When current output is less than normal output, a lower value of δ may be expected because of the technical and economic disadvantages of scrapping existing capital, and because any downward movement of output is likely to be contrary to its trend and thus may be quickly reversed. For practical applications of the theory, different values of the coefficients may be required for different stages in the economic cycle.

Chenery's capital stock adjustment model related only to net investment, and took no explicit account of expectations about future output. A theory of gross investment which also accounts for 'expectational' investment has been presented by de Leeuw (1962). His approach is to distinguish three separate components of gross investment:
  (i) projects needed to offset the continual wearing out of the existing capital stock—replacement investment.
  (ii) projects needed to bring capacity into its optimum relationship with current output—adjustment investment.
  (iii) projects needed to take account of expected changes in output —expectational investment.
Provided that each of these can be specified in terms of expenditure requirements, a composite variable 'capital requirements' can be

83 ibid., p. 12.

obtained, and this in turn defines the investment which it induces. The theory of replacement investment has already been discussed in ch. 2 § 7, and that of expectations in the previous section. The investment required to restore an optimum capacity-output relationship can be specified by

$$I^A = f(K^* - K), \qquad (2.16)$$

where I^A is investment required for adjustment purposes, and K^* is that level of capital stock which is optimum given the current situation. The optimum, or desired capital stock, may be specified as in Jorgenson's version of the neoclassical theory. Assuming that the level of capital services supplied is proportional to the size of the capital stock, the desired capital stock is that at which the marginal productivity of capital is equal to its net rental value, or user cost. Unfortunately, application of this theory requires data on the prices of capital goods and the internal rates of discount used by firms, neither of which are easily available. Moreover, the implicit assumptions of rationality, profit-maximisation and certainty concerning the future (let alone the present) conflict both with one's own experience of the real world and with much of the survey evidence reported in ch. 3 § 2. Most business-men are neither unemotional nor mathematically agile, and although the Jorgenson version of the neoclassical theory may nevertheless describe the results of their behaviour, it seems preferable to formulate a theory more in accord with their actual decision-making processes. Moreover, even if the Jorgenson model provides an accurate description of the investment behaviour of individual firms, it is doubtful whether its highly non-linear form can meaningfully bear aggregation to the macro level.

An alternative is to assume that the desired capital stock is simply a function of the rate of output. For example, assuming that there is some optimal rate of aggregate capital utilisation (λ), the optimal capital stock may be defined as that which, if used at the optimal rate, would equate the capital stock then utilised with the existing stock in use (K):

thus $$\lambda K^* = K \quad \text{and} \quad K^* = \frac{K}{\lambda}. \qquad (2.17)$$

If λ can be presumed constant, this specification requires data on only the capital stock actually in use. In regression analysis the value of λ will be incorporated in the regression coefficient.

Estimates of the capital stock actually in use can be obtained by multiplying the existing stock of capital by the rate of capital utilisation. Unfortunately the measurement of capital utilisation presents consider-able problems and statistical series are not readily available. Since

January 1968, a regular quarterly series on the rate of capacity utilisation in the United States has been published in the Federal Reserve Bulletin.[84] However a clear distinction must be drawn between the rate of capital utilisation—the unemployment rate of the capital stock—and the rate of capacity utilisation which, based on comparisons of actual output and 'full capacity' output, relates to the utilisation of all factors of production. That this is so is clear from an examination of two alternative methods of measuring capacity utilisation which have been described by Klein and Summers (1967) and Klein and Preston (1968). The method described by Klein and Summers is that employed by the Wharton School Econometrics Unit in their model of the U.S. economy. A simple set of rules is used to identify cyclical peaks in output and then, on the assumption that these peaks occurred at times of full capacity utilisation, a series for 'full capacity output' is obtained by interpolating between them. Capacity utilisation in each period is then calculated by expressing actual output as a percentage of full capacity output. The Wharton Index of Capacity Utilisation is a weighted average of the results of applying the above method to 36 separate industries. The alternative method described by Klein and Preston involves fitting production functions to industry data on output and labour and capital services. The estimated coefficients are then used to compute the rates of output that would have been achieved in each industry if the existing labour forces and capital stocks had always been fully employed. The industry rates of capacity utilisation in each period are obtained by expressing their actual outputs as percentages of their calculated potential outputs, and the aggregate rate is again calculated as a weighted average of the separate industry rates. Thus both methods relate actual output to 'full capacity' output rather than the capital stock in use to the existing capital stock. Indeed the method described by Klein and Preston requires the rate of capital utilisation to be assumed equal to that of labour utilisation!

The approach of relating capital utilisation to labour utilisation is, however, potentially fruitful. Although the two rates have been equated by Klein and Preston and by Solow (1957), a curvilinear relationship such that capital utilisation shows greater variation than labour utilisation seems more appropriate. For example, a logarithmic function[85]

84 This is based on data supplied by the McGraw-Hill Dept. of Economics, the Federal Reserve System and the Dept. of Commerce. An appraisal of separate series constructed by McGraw-Hill, the Federal Reserve System, the National Industrial Conference Board and the Wharton School Econometrics Unit has been provided by Phillips (1963).

85 This assumption was used by St. Cyr (1964).

may be assumed between capital utilisation and labour employment, such that

$$\frac{K}{\bar{K}} = (1-u)^{\gamma} \qquad (2.18)$$

where u is the unemployment rate and γ is a constant. The coefficient γ can be estimated by fitting a production function of the conventional Cobb-Douglas type

$$Y = A\,K^{\alpha}\,L^{\beta}\,e^{rt} \qquad (2.19)$$

to time-series data on the firms/industries/economy under study. For purposes of estimation the production function can then be expressed as

$$Y = A\,\bar{K}^{\alpha}\,(1-u)^{\alpha\gamma}\,L^{\beta}\,e^{rt} \qquad (2.20)$$

and hence as

$$\log Y = \log A + \alpha \log \bar{K} + \alpha\gamma \log(1-u) + \beta \log L + rt \qquad (2.21)$$

and the estimate of γ derived by dividing that of $\alpha\gamma$ by that of α. Unfortunately besides the doubts concerning the theoretical validity of aggregate production functions, this method is subject to serious statistical problems. In particular, multicollinearity between aggregate output, capital stock, employment, and the time trend results in co-efficients with high sampling errors and sometimes incorrect signs.

Another possible approach to the measurement of capital utilisation is that of asking direct questions about the topic in regular surveys of business trends and opinion. The U.S. index of capacity utilisation now published in the Federal Reserve Bulletin is based on information from three sources. One of these is the McGraw-Hill Survey of Business' Plans for New Plants and Equipment which include questions on capacity 'measured in terms of physical volume' and the rate at which companies are actually operating. A similar question, but one which requires only a yes/no answer is asked in the four-monthly industrial trends surveys conducted by the Confederation of British Industry. Firms are simply asked whether or not their present output is below capacity (i.e., a satisfactorily full rate of operation).

Although both this question and that asked in the McGraw-Hill surveys appear to relate to capacity rather than capital utilisation, a recent survey by Glynn (1969) of 39 respondents to the C.B.I. enquiry found that the majority thought primarily in terms of the capacity of their plant. Thus a regular survey question worded specifically in terms of plant capacity may be capable of producing a meaningful series on capital utilisation. Although the percentage of firms fully utilising their capital stock is not the same as the aggregate rate of capital utilisation, the correlation between the two may be sufficiently high for the former to serve as a proxy for the latter.

One of the major problems in capital stock adjustment models is therefore that of specifying, and subsequently calculating, the desired capital stock. However, the incorporation of the adjustment process, and separate and explicit provision for both replacement and expectational investment does represent a major advance on the crude acceleration principle. Two further modifications are required to enhance the claims of capital stock adjustment models to be acceptable theories of aggregate investment. First, they ignore the influence of financial factors, especially the availability of internal funds and the cost of external funds. Secondly, since the investment process takes time—often a considerable period of time—it is necessary for a satisfactory theory of aggregate investment to incorporate the complex lag structure involved. Several possible ways of tackling the first problem are outlined in the remainder of this section, consideration of the second being postponed until the final section of this chapter.

The incorporation of financial variables into capital stock adjustment models has generally followed one of two alternative approaches. The first is that typified by Jorgenson's version of the neoclassical theory, in which on the basis of certain rather strict assumptions, some financial variables play a precise role in the determination of the optimum capital stock. The second is that of many econometric studies of investment: an assortment of financial variables is added to the list of possible explanatory variables for experimentation in linear regression analysis. Neither is wholly satisfactory.

In a recent study of quarterly capital expenditure in Canada, Evans and Helliwell (1969) consider four alternative ways, including the two above, in which financial variables might properly be incorporated into a theory of aggregate investment. Firstly, financial factors may play some part in the determination of the desired capital stock, though this role might not accord with the strictly rational and profit-maximising assumptions implicit in the neoclassical theory. The next two specifications imply that, for any given discrepancy between the desired and actual capital stocks, the pace of adjustment—the rate of investment— is determined by financial factors. One assumes that the reaction of firms to any positive gap is faster the more favourable are financial factors; the other assumes that the actual gestation period for capital goods will be less the more favourable are these factors. The final specification is eclectic: it may be that financial variables are clearly important in the determination of aggregate investment, but their precise impact cannot be specified in a satisfactory manner. Rather than exclude them from a model of aggregate investment, it is clearly preferable to include them in a linear relationship as a reasonable first approximation.

The results of regression analysis led the authors to conclude that the first specification is appropriate for Canadian investment in non-residential construction, but only the latter for investment in machinery and equipment.

2.10. Tax Incentives and Disincentives to Investment

Because of the importance of investment in determining both the rate of growth of, and fluctuations in, national income, governments have increasingly sought to regulate the level of investment demand. This attempt has largely found expression through a variety of tax schemes to stimulate investment. As Eckstein (1962) commented:[86]

'Tax devices to stimulate investment have certainly been the greatest fad in economic policy in the past ten years. In a period when the trends in the use of policy instruments were in the direction of more general, less selective devices, all sorts of liberalised depreciation schemes, investment allowances, and tax exemptions were embraced with enthusiasm all over the non-Communist world.'

However, as Hall and Jorgenson (1967) noted:[87]

'the belief in the efficacy of tax stimulus does not rely on empirical evidence . . . (but) . . . is based on the plausible argument that businessmen will find the purchase of capital goods more attractive if they cost less.'

In fact the extent to which businessmen do respond to tax incentives to invest has been the subject of some controversy. Hall and Jorgenson attempted to assess the effectiveness of the United States tax provisions, but unfortunately the value of their results is somewhat reduced by the restrictive nature of their assumptions. Following the approach described on pp. 31–33, they implicitly assumed that businessmen take full and complete account of the incentives when deciding upon their desired capital stock, and since they found that investment is sensitive to changes in the desired capital stock, they were bound to conclude that the incentives were effective. The crucial question, however, is whether or not businessmen are responsive to tax incentives; do they influence their desired capital stock?

As the specific type of tax incentives used to stimulate investment vary from country to country, and moreover within each country change from time to time, a fairly typical system of incentives will be used to describe the accounting principles involved and the manner in which the

86 Eckstein (1962), p. 351.
87 Hall and Jorgenson (1967), p. 391.

incentives might be incorporated into a theory of aggregate investment. The system chosen as an example is that which was operative in the United Kingdom throughout the post-war period up to the introduction of Corporation Tax in 1966.

The tax allowances available in the United Kingdom during this period were of four types: 'annual', 'initial', 'investment' and 'balancing'. The annual allowance was the amount by which a firm could depreciate its assets each year for tax purposes, the amount of the allowance then being set as a cost against the firm's tax liability. Assets were depreciated according to either the 'reducing balance' or 'straight-line' methods. Under the reducing balance method, an asset is depreciated each year by a fixed proportion of its written-down value at the end of the preceding year; whereas under the straight-line method, the annual depreciation is a fixed proportion of the asset's initial cost. In each case, the proportions were specified for each type of asset, and were dependent on the usual lifetime of that asset. The scheme of initial allowances was introduced in 1945, and was intended as a method of accelerated depreciation. The proportion of an asset's cost which could be set against tax in the year of purchase was increased by the amount of the initial allowance. However, correspondingly less was allowed in the subsequent years of the asset's life. The scheme of investment allowances was introduced in 1954, and was intended to represent a permanent exemption from taxation. Again the proportion of an asset's cost which could be set against tax in the first year was increased by the amount of the allowance, but unlike the initial allowances, the investment allowances did not reduce the amount of future tax allowable depreciation. Although the investment allowances were originally introduced as an alternative to the initial allowances, the two types of allowances existed concurrently during the period 1959–66. The purpose of the balancing allowance was to provide for the eventuality of an asset being sold or scrapped, and its owner receiving a price different from its written-down value. In such a case an adjustment was made 'to ensure that the initial and annual allowances previously made are either augmented or reduced so that the total allowances finally made will correspond with the net cost of the (asset) to the trader'.[88]

The effects that the initial and investment allowances—the ones primarily considered as policy instruments—were likely to have on firms' investment decisions was often the subject of controversy. The initial allowance was frequently characterised as 'a temporary interest-free loan: the loan is gradually reduced because the annual allowances

88 The Board of Inland Revenue (1963), pp. 7–8.

for subsequent years are lower than they would have been in the absence of initial allowances'.[89] On the other hand, it was argued that 'since only a small proportion of investment is accounted for by static firms which possess a single asset or which exhibit a marked replacement cycle, it is more realistic to regard investment as a continuing process; the "loan" represented by initial allowances will then "revolve" as new assets are purchased'.[90] Other characteristics of the allowances that were stressed were that 'the remission given . . . is reclaimable only against future tax'[91] and that they were 'available to a business . . . regardless of its borrowing powers'.[92] The former of these characteristics increased the risk element in investment, while the latter was likely to be particularly important to firms which experienced difficulty in obtaining finance. Clearly both the initial and investment allowances could be considered as either sources of funds or as subsidies since they raised the prospective rate of return.

The profitability aspect of the system of investment, initial and annual allowances was examined by Merrett and Sykes (1963). We shall denote the initial cost of a capital good by C, its lifetime by n, the annual allowance by w, the initial allowance by u, the investment allowance by v, the rate of time discount by d, the tax rate on profits by T, and the lag in tax payments by g. If an asset is depreciated according to the reducing balance method, and the firm chooses to write the asset down indefinitely, the present value of the series of allowances is

$$\frac{(v+u+w)\ TC}{(1+d)^g}+\frac{w(1-u-w)\ TC}{(1+d)^{g+1}}+\frac{w(1-u-w)\ (1-w)\ TC}{(1+d)^{g+2}}$$

$$+\frac{w(1-u-w)\ (1-w)^2\ TC}{(1+d)^{g+3}}+\ \ldots+\frac{w(1-u-w)\ (1-w)^i\ TC}{(1+d)^{g+i+1}}+\ldots$$

$$=\frac{(v+u+w)\ TC}{(1+d)^g}+\sum_{i=0}^{i=\infty}\frac{w(1-u-w)\ (1-w)^i\ TC}{(1+d)^{g+i+1}}$$

$$=\frac{TC}{(1+d)^g}\left[(v+u+w)+\frac{w(1-u-w)}{(d+w)}\right]. \tag{2.22}$$

Hence the present value of the allowances as a proportion of the cost of the capital good is

$$\frac{T}{(1+d)^g}\left[(v+u+w)+\frac{w(1-u-w)}{(d+w)}\right]. \tag{2.23}$$

89 H.M.S.O. (1951), para. 117.
90 Sumner (1966), p. 352.
91 H.M.S.O. (1955), para. 428.
92 ibid., para. 428.

If an asset is depreciated according to the straight-line method, the present value of the series of allowances is

$$\frac{(v+u+w)\,TC}{(1+d)^g}+\frac{w\,TC}{(1+d)^{g+1}}+\frac{w\,TC}{(1+d)^{g+2}}+\cdots+\frac{w\,TC}{(1+d)^{g+n}}$$

where

$$n=\frac{1-u-w}{w},$$

the number of subsequent years over which the firm can claim annual allowances. The present value of the series of allowances is thus

$$\frac{(v+u+w)\,TC}{(1+d)^g}+\sum_{i=0}^{i=n-1}\frac{w\,TC}{(1+d)^{g+i+1}}$$

$$=\frac{TC}{(1+d)^g}\left[(v+u+w)+\frac{w(1+d)^n-w}{d(1+d)^n}\right], \tag{2.24}$$

and expressed as a proportion of the cost of the capital good their value is

$$\frac{T}{(1+d)^g}\left[(v+u+w)+\frac{w(1+d)^n-w}{d(1+d)^n}\right]. \tag{2.25}$$

One or other of equations (2.22), (2.24) can be incorporated into the criteria for project evaluation expressed in ch. 2 § 7, to provide a rational basis for assessing investment for which the tax allowances are available. For an investment to be profitable, it is necessary only for the present value of the expected annual returns to exceed the cost of the capital good net of the present value of the tax allowances. However, as a theory of investment behaviour, this decision rule is subject to all the criticisms of the theory of optimal capital accumulation outlined in ch. 2 § 4. Moreover, firms may ignore such allowances because of frequent changes in their magnitude, because of the necessity of earning profits in the future to benefit from them, and because their value depends on future rates of taxation.[93]

Indeed the assumptions of profit-maximisation and employment of the discounted cash flow technique of investment appraisal upon which the above analysis is based may themselves be invalid. Evidence that this is the case, at least within the context of the United Kingdom

93 For an exposition of these arguments see C.B.I. (1965), para 15, and H.M.S.O. (1966), para. 15.

economy during the period for which the above system was effective, is provided by the findings of various interview and questionnaire studies reported in ch. 3 § 2. However, although firms may not take full account of a system of incentives, it does not follow that the system has no effect at all. How then can provision for such a situation be made in a theory of aggregate investment, particularly one designed for subsequent econometric application?

One possibility is to consider both the investment and initial allowances as separate determinants of aggregate investment, and include them as separate explanatory variables in a linear regression formulation. Unfortunately this approach may raise problems of multicollinearity and limit the available number of degrees of freedom to an extent unlikely to be justified by the importance of the allowances. Another possible approach is that adopted by Balapoulos (1967) who constructed a weighted average of the two allowances, the weights being determined on 'a priori' grounds. The relative value of the investment and initial allowances has been compared by Black (1959) for the case of straight-line depreciation using some very simple assumptions about the effective timing of the allowances. He showed that the value of an investment allowance was greater relative to that of an equal initial allowance the shorter was the expected length of an asset's life and the lower was the subjective rate of interest. Since interview and questionnaire studies have shown that most United Kingdom firms consider the returns which are expected from an investment project during only the first few years of its life, and that they require high rates of return, firms probably valued the investment allowances much more than the initial allowances. Consequently a weighted average of the two allowances should give the greater weight to the investment allowance. Alternative 'a priori' reasonable sets of weights may be specified, and the choice between them determined by their performance in regression analysis.

Businessmen often claim that the level of company taxation is a deterrent to innovation and investment. There are two major aspects to their arguments. Firstly, that a high rate of taxation on profits reduces the amount of profits available for investment; secondly, that by reducing the rewards to successful risk-taking it has strong disincentive effects. The first argument has relevance only if investment is a function of the level of profits. The second argument has strong intuitive appeal, but the following criticism of it has been made by Carter and Williams (1957):[94]

94 Carter and Williams (1957), p. 149.

'Profits retained or capital borrowed by companies have got to be employed somehow; and if new processes are going unadopted because of high taxation, where are the alternative and superior ways of using profits which are so attractive? The tax-gatherer is round every corner, and this fact leaves the choice to be made on relative and not on absolute yields.'

However their argument is erroneous in that choices are made on absolute and not on relative yields. It is the size of the absolute difference in expected yields between two alternative forms of investment which an individual should weigh against the differences in the risk attached to them. A reduction in absolute yields does reduce the appeal of new innovations and those types of investment which offer prospective high yields but are subject to considerable risk.

Unfortunately human nature makes it difficult to achieve a logical and unbiased assessment of the effects of personal and also company taxation. Everyone would like to pay less tax, and arguments that personal satisfaction is consistent with the social good are obviously very attractive. Consequently they may be accepted too readily. On the other hand, a psychological belief in the disincentive effects of high tax rates may itself create these disincentive effects. As Carter and Williams rightly commented:[95]

'a reduction in taxation might alter the climate of opinion so that business thinks it has a greater incentive to invest, even though it is difficult to trace the exact reasons for that opinion'.

2.11. Time Lags

The need for an explicit recognition of time lags in the formulation of a theory of investment can be illustrated by considering first the lags which affect a single capital expenditure undertaken by an individual firm. The total lag between the time when the firm is faced with a situation in which it requires further capital expenditure and the actual expenditure (investment) consists of the following components:

(i) The time which elapses between the situations stimulating the purchase of capital goods and the firm's knowledge about the situations. This is the time lag caused by the collection and provision of the relevant statistical information relating to the firm, its industry, and the economy as a whole.

95 ibid., p. 150.

(ii) The time taken by the management of the firm to draft plans for the proposed capital project, to decide on its advisability, and to arrange the necessary finance.

(iii) The time taken by the firm to make its decision effective. This involves either an outright purchase, or (for most types of capital goods), the placing of an order.

(iv) For capital goods supplied to order, there may be a further lag before the work on them commences; this is referred to as the queuing period. This lag will exist only if the industries producing the required capital goods are working fairly close to capacity, and its length is likely to depend on the current pressure of demand for capital goods.

(v) For capital goods supplied to order, there will also be a lag between the start of work and their production. In some cases, the actual capital expenditure will be made by the firm only when the goods are delivered; in other cases, capital expenditure—in the form of progress payments—will be being made by the firm at intervals during the production period.

Summing these components, the total lag between the situation requiring capital expenditure and the actual expenditure is seen to consist of a fixed, and in many cases, a distributed component. A further distributed lag effect is introduced if the firm, instead of responding to a situation existing at a single point in time (as assumed above), is more cautious and determines its policy with respect to a spectrum of its recent experiences. The total length of the lag is not easily predicted on 'a priori' grounds. However, for capital goods which are built to order, and for which progress payments are not made, the fixed component of the lag distribution cannot be less than their minimum production period.

When considering the lag distribution relevant to all the capital expenditures undertaken by a single firm, the problem becomes more complex. Even for decisions made at the same point in time, different lags are likely to be associated with different capital goods, because of differences in their queuing and production periods. Moreover the decision-making time may vary with the magnitude of the expenditure involved. The consideration of capital expenditure decisions at a more aggregate level (industry or whole economy) introduces additional complications to the lag scheme, since different firms may have different speeds of response to any given situation, and they are likely to require different assortments of capital goods. Finally, the introduction of the time dimension further complicates the lag scheme since, for each firm and for each type of capital good, the information, decision-making, ordering, queuing, and production period components of the lag structure may change over time. Variations in the first three are likely to be determined by such factors as changes in the internal organisation and complexity of individual firms, and developments in data collection and provision. Variations in production periods are likely to be caused by both trend and cyclical influences: the trend influence reflecting changes in the production techniques, and the increasing complexity of capital goods; while the cyclical influence is attributable to swings in the pressure of demand on the capital goods industries. This latter influence is also likely to determine both the existence of, and length of, the queuing period.

Chapter 3

STATISTICAL AND QUESTIONNAIRE STUDIES

Empirical studies of investment may be classified in the following manner:

(i)   statistical studies; these seek to describe trends and variations in investment, and characterise some of the major features of the investment process, without attempting to explain its determination.

(ii) interview and questionnaire studies of the rationale and factors influencing the investment decisions made by individual firms.

(iii) econometric studies of investment conducted at the micro level.

(iv) econometric studies of investment conducted at the macro level.

Statistical studies of aggregate investment often provide valuable information about the institutional framework within which the investment process takes place, and identify the movements in investment which the other types of studies seek to explain. Following the methodological approach of developing a macro level theory of investment distinct from, but necessarily related to, theories about the investment behaviour of micro units, the second and third types of studies provide some clues as to the correct specification of the aggregate investment function, whilst studies of the fourth type yield more explicit guidance.

The methodology and results of statistical and questionnaire studies are discussed in this chapter, and the conclusions of regression analysis are examined in ch. 5. As the majority of the regression studies relate to United States experience, the discussion of the other types of studies will focus mainly on those relating to the United Kingdom. However, in the case of both countries an attempt will be made to compare and reconcile the findings of the two types of studies.

3.1. Statistical Studies

The description in ch. 1 § 2.3 of the major features of, and trends in, fixed investment in the United Kingdom and the United States typifies many statistical studies. A similar study, relating to United Kingdom manufacturing industry during the period 1948–62 was presented in the May 1963 issue of the Central Statistical Office publication, Economic Trends. In addition this study analysed and compared the data for individual industries and businesses within manufacturing industry. It was discovered that 'although each industry shows a rhythmical pattern of alternating rises and falls of (capital) expenditure in which the influence of the overall picture is discernible, the individual cycles have by no means uniform patterns or intensities'.[1] Moreover, this same diversity was found between the capital expenditures of individual large businesses within the same industry; it was not uncommon for the investment of particular businesses to move counter-cyclically. It was stated that this finding may be explained by 'the many different influences upon the investment policies of the individual firm, for example, modernisation, technical development, expanding markets, pressure of competition, deployment of liquid assets and new management'.[2] The diversity of investment expenditure between industries and between businesses does appear to indicate that the important factors affecting investment decisions may be ones which are specific to individual firms and not ones experienced by all firms in common. However, such a conclusion, and indeed all conclusions based on similar observations from statistical studies, can only be stated very tentatively since they cannot be readily subjected to statistical testing. In particular, given that the capital expenditures of different businesses can never be expected to show exactly the same pattern, what criteria can be employed to indicate whether any significance can be attached to their observed diversity? When is diversity too diverse? Moreover, even if one accepts the explanation that different influences operate to determine the capital expenditures undertaken by different firms, it does not follow that there are no influences which affect all firms in the same way and which may be of prime importance in the determination of aggregate investment. The usefulness of such studies is therefore very much open to question.

Statistical studies of the sources and uses of funds by firms can shed considerable light on the relative importance of different sources of funds in the financing of investment. Several sets of such statistics have been published in the United Kingdom. A consistent series, based on

1 Economic Trends (May 1963), p. iii.
2 ibid., p. iv.

the published accounts of industrial and commercial companies whose shares are quoted on the United Kingdom stock exchanges, has been made available for the period 1949–60. A summarised version of this series is included in table 3.1. For clarity, years have been grouped into successive 4-year periods, and the relative importance of each source and use of funds highlighted by expressing each as a percentage. Table 3.1 also presents a comparison of the relative sources and uses of quoted and non-quoted companies in the years 1960–62. The major source of funds for the quoted companies was clearly the retention of profits (additions to company reserves and provisions for depreciation, etc.), though various types of direct borrowing raised between 18·6% and 31·5% of the total available funds in the different periods. For these firms the importance of external funds and in particular ordinary share issues increased throughout the period. Their most important use of funds was expenditure on tangible fixed assets, i.e. fixed investment. Unfortunately the table does not permit a breakdown of the sources of funds for the financing of fixed investment alone. Since long-term loans and share issues are probably used to finance fixed investment rather than for more general purposes,[3] it is likely that the percentage of investment financed in this way was higher than the 14·8–26·9% suggested by the figures in the table.

The 1960–62 data on non-quoted companies was obtained in a survey undertaken to examine 'the differences in the pattern of financing between quoted companies and fairly large companies which do not have direct access to the capital market rather than between large and small companies'.[4] Despite this intention, the average size of the companies in the sample of non-quoted companies was considerably less than that of the quoted companies, and consequently the differences in the sources of funds may reflect differences in company size as well as different opportunities to raise funds on the capital market. The major apparent difference between the sources of funds of the two types of companies was that the non-quoted companies relied far less on long-term financing, and in particular on share issues, and far more on 'other credit', particularly trade credit. However, part of this difference may be explained by the different uses to which the quoted and non-quoted companies put their funds. The increase in the value of stocks and in credit extended, neither of which are likely to be financed by share issues, accounted for 43·1% of the funds of non-quoted companies compared to only 28·3% of the funds of quoted companies. Another

3 Support for this assertion is provided by the results of a survey conducted and reported by the Federation of British Industries (1960).
4 Economic Trends (Feb., 1965), p. ii.

TABLE 3.1

Sources and uses of funds of United Kingdom industrial and commercial companies, 1949–62

	Percentages for quoted companies in successive 4-year periods			Percentages for quoted and non-quoted companies 1960–62	
	1949–52	1953–56	1957–60	Quoted	Non-quoted
Sources of funds					
Receipts from issues of long term loans	6·3	6·5	4·8	7·0	2·8
Receipts from issues of ordinary shares	6·9	8·8	15·0	18·9	4·8
Receipts from issues of preference, etc., shares	1·6	1·5	1·2	1·0	0·1
Increase in amounts owing to banks	3·8	2·7	4·3	6·6	11·8
Increase in other (mainly trade) credit	18·8	16·6	14·0	12·0	27·3
Additions to company reserves and provisions for depreciation, etc.	62·3	60·3	58·2	51·0	51·5
Other sources	4·3	3·6	2·5	3·5	1·7
Uses of funds					
Expenditure on tangible fixed assets	39·8	52·5	55·5	57·6	57·1
Expenditure on trade investments, goodwill and other intangibles	1·8	1·3	3·8	6·2	0·4
Increase in value of stocks	28·9	18·8	13·3	15·8	25·4
Increase in trade and other debtors	18·1	15·8	14·8	12·5	17·7
Other uses	8·5	10·1	10·5	12·2	4·2
Balancing items (mainly increase in holdings of cash, marketable securities and tax reserve certificates)	2·9	1·5	2·1	−4·3	−4·8

Note: Total sources of funds = total uses of funds.

Source: For quoted companies, 1949–60, the April 1962 issue of the Central Statistical Office publication Economic Trends. For quoted and non-quoted companies 1960–62, Economic Trends (Feb. 1965).

difficulty of comparison is that since 202 of the 460 non-quoted companies in the sample were subsidiaries of or controlled by overseas companies, much of the 'other credit' may represent financing by overseas parent companies—a source of funds not available to most non-quoted companies.

TABLE 3.2

Sources and uses of funds of United Kingdom industrial and
commercial companies, 1963–67

	% of total
Sources of funds	
Undistributed income before providing for depreciation, stock appreciation and additions to reserves	73·1
Capital transfers (net)	1·4
Bank lending	10·9
Other loans and mortgages	3·5
Capital issues (net) by quoted companies of which:	
Ordinary shares	2·7
Debenture and preference shares	8·4
Total	100·0
Uses of funds	
Gross domestic fixed capital formation	57·4
Increase in value of stocks and work in progress	12·0
Liquid assets, including bank deposits	7·4
Acquisition of subsidiaries and trade investments in the U.K. and overseas	10·0
Acquisition of other overseas assets	3·9
Unidentified items (residual)	9·3
Total	100·0

Note: Total sources of funds = total uses of funds.
Source: Sept. 1968 issue of the Central Statistical Office publication
Financial Statistics.

Since February 1965, the publication Financial Statistics has included a continuing series on the sources and uses of the funds of industrial and commercial companies. The series has a very comprehensive coverage, accounting for almost 95 % of all gross fixed capital formation by companies. A summarised version of the series for 1963–67 is presented in table 3.2, showing the percentage share of each source and use of funds in the total. Undistributed income is clearly the major source of funds, although bank lending and debenture and preference shares are also important. Unfortunately the figures presented in table 3.2 are not directly comparable with those presented in table 3.1 because of differing classifications and differing coverage. Thus the apparent increases in the importance of undistributed income and bank lending and decrease in the importance of ordinary share issues may be partly explained by the inclusion of many smaller companies in the new series.

TABLE 3.3

Sources and uses of funds of United States nonfarm nonfinancial corporate business, 1956–67

	Percentages for successive 4-year periods		
	1956–59	1960–63	1964–67
Sources of funds			
Undistributed profits, including corporate inventory valuation adjustment	21·9	19·9	23·1
Capital consumption allowances	44·4	47·4	41·8
Stocks	4·8	1·9	1·2
Bonds	9·9	7·2	9·9
Mortgages	1·7	3·9	3·5
Bank and other loans	4·9	4·0	9·5
Trade debt	8·2	8·7	6·5
Other liabilities	4·2	7·0	4·5
Total	100·0	100·0	100·0
Uses of funds			
Nonresidential fixed investment	66·1	62·2	62·8
Residential structures	2·3	4·4	3·9
Change in business inventories	3·8	5·8	9·3
Increase in liquid assets	2·0	3·5	1·5
Consumer and trade credit	14·5	15·1	13·1
Other financial assets	6·8	7·4	6·3
Discrepancy (uses less sources)	4·5	1·6	3·1
Total	100·0	100·0	100·0

Note: Total sources of funds = total uses of funds.
Source: Economic Report of the President, transmitted to the Congress, January 1968.

Statistical information on the sources and uses of the funds of United States nonfarm nonfinancial corporations is published in the Annual Report of the President. The percentage importance of each source and use during three successive four-year periods, 1956–67, is shown in table 3.3. Internal sources are clearly of prime importance, providing approximately two-thirds of all funds. As in the case of the United Kingdom industrial and commercial companies, external long-term financing provides only about 10% of all funds, of which only a very small part is raised by the issue of ordinary stocks. Nonresidential fixed investment is clearly the major use of funds. The overall picture that emerges from table 3.3 is one of constancy through time, with little apparent difference existing between the sources and uses of funds of United Kingdom and United States companies.

There are various problems associated with using data such as presented in tables 3.1–3.3 to indicate the influence which the availabilities of different sources of finance has on investment. Firstly, as already stated, the tables show the sources of funds for all purposes, not merely for the financing of fixed investment. It is impossible to construct statistics showing the financing of fixed investment alone, since companies do not apportion particular sources of funds to particular purposes. Secondly, the sources of funds which are most important in total may not be the most important in marginal investment decisions. For example, although retained profits may finance most investment, marginal investment decisions, and hence variations in total investment, may be dependent upon the possibility of, and costs of, equity issues.

Statistical studies have, however, been of more assistance in examining the time lags to which the investment process is subject, and especially the cyclical variations in these lags. Zarnowitz (1962), in a study of the response of business to fluctuations in the volume of orders received, considered three possible alternative or complementary responses: (i) increases and decreases in the current output and/or price, (ii) depletions and replenishments of inventory of the product, (iii) accumulations and decumulations of the order backlog. Although the first type of response has received considerable theoretical analysis, Zarnowitz argued that some of the basic ingredients of economic life—uncertainty, lags of adjustments, cost of change as a function of size and frequency of change—make it more likely that stocks and order backlog would be used as adjustment instruments or shock absorbers. That this is so in the case of United States durable goods industries is confirmed by the variations in the unfilled orders/sales ratio between cyclical peaks shown in table 3.4. Since this ratio is indicative of the length of the queuing plus production periods, it follows that the lag was greatest at the cyclical peaks and least at the cyclical troughs. The extent to which variations in this ratio, and hence in the queuing plus production periods, resulted in a flow of both production and shipments much smoother than that of new orders is shown in table 3.5. The average amplitude in new orders of all durable goods was almost twice that of production and shipments, and for no industry group were either production or shipments more volatile than new orders. This finding was confirmed by Popkin (1965) who studied United States data on machinery and equipment purchases.

TABLE 3.4

Peak and trough ratios of unfilled orders to monthly sales in United States durable-goods industries, 1946–59

Date	Peak/trough	Ratio
Feb., 1946	Peak	5·99
Sept., 1949	Trough	2·41
July, 1952	Peak	7·72
May, 1955	Trough	3·51
July, 1956	Peak	4·54
June, 1959	Trough	2·98

Source: Zarnowitz (1962), table 1, p. 368.

TABLE 3.5

Amplitude and timing of new orders, production and shipments in major United States durable goods industries, 1948–58

	Average relative amplitude of cyclical movements			Average lag between new orders and production (months)
	New orders	Production	Shipments	
Total durable goods	38	20	20	7·1
Primary metals	51	47	48	4·1
Fabricated metal products	47	17	19	3·5
Electrical machinery	50	26	34	1·7
Nonelectrical machinery	42	28	32	3·3
Motor vehicles and parts	57	41	39	3·3
Nonautomotive transport equipment	197	71	70	9·7
Other durable goods	27	17	16	0·7

Note: For each successive expansion and contraction in the given series, the amplitude was measured between the average levels of the series in the three-month period centred on the initial and terminal turns. All amplitudes were expressed in percentages of the initial-term levels. The figures above represent averages of the expansion and contraction amplitudes taken without regard to sign.

Source: Zarnowitz (1962), table 7, p. 388.

Statistical information on the average construction times of United Kingdom industrial buildings has been provided by the analysis of Lund (1967). He showed that not only was the rate of completion of industrial buildings more smooth than that of starts, but that estimates of the actual flow of work done were less volatile than either starts or completions. The consequence of this smoothing of new demand was that average construction times varied markedly over the cycle—ranging from about 17 to about 28 months during the period 1950–64. A similar examination of machine tool data[5] revealed even greater relative variation: the average lag between order and delivery being as low as 6 months and as high as 14 months during the period 1956–66.

3.2. Interview and Questionnaire Studies

Interview and questionnaire studies of the investment process in individual firms have usually been directed towards one or other of two objectives. Some have sought to establish the criteria used by firms when assessing prospective investment projects. Such studies have delved into the origins of a project's history, the intra-firm discussions concerning their advisability, and the basic motivating forces underlying firms' decision-making processes. Others have attempted to determine the influence which particular economic variables have had on firms' investment decisions. In particular, attention has been concentrated on the importance of interest rates and of tax allowances designed to stimulate aggregate investment. Most of the published empirical studies of United Kingdom investment have been of the interview/questionnaire type, and they will be reviewed first. A detailed critical review of several United States studies has been presented by Eisner (1957), and so the discussion of the American literature will be less comprehensive.

Several studies of the investment motivation and criteria of United Kingdom firms have been conducted in recent years, notably by Barna (1962), Neild (1964), Williams and Scott (1965), Mackintosh (1963) and N.E.D.C. (1965). Barna's study was based on an analysis of the published accounts of, and interviews with the managements of, medium-sized companies in the electrical engineering and food processing industries. The selected sample consisted of 81 firms, but interviews were held with representatives of only 35 companies. The person interviewed was usually a member of the company's board of directors, or an official with constant access to it—such as the company secretary or chief

5 This was presented in an unpublished Ph.D. Thesis 'United Kingdom Investment in Industrial Buildings and Machine Tools: An Econometric Study'. University of Manchester, 1969.

accountant. No questionnaires were used, but an attempt was made to collect information systematically. Barna considered that although the results of the interviews were consistent with the hypothesis that profit maximisation is an underlying motive of business behaviour and in particular of investment decisions, they also suggested other motives which may conflict with the profit motive. The chief of these was found to be the desire for growth; Barna reported that 'each firm wants to become bigger in terms of turnover, capital and profits'.[6] The external pressures to investment—technical change, increase in demand, competition, market saturation—were said to become effective only if the firm had an underlying desire for growth. Despite this desire for growth, only 14 of the 35 firms had plans for periods ranging from two to five years; planning, especially in a formal manner, was not prevalent amongst the larger firms. Analysis of the interviews also suggested that the criteria used for assessing investment projects may vary according to the type of project. In particular, larger firms were often found to decentralise decisions concerning replacement investment, and a lower minimum rate of profit was often required for replacement investment than for other projects. One-third of the firms did not require written evidence when the profitability of an investment project was being assessed. In general firms were found to be reluctant to raise long-term debt or to borrow from a bank, though the preference for internal funds appeared to be less strong amongst the larger firms. Finally, the study suggested that short-term fluctuations in investment are (at least in part) the result of changes in business confidence:[7]

'Businessmen sometimes claim that they are not affected by day-to-day events or by short-term changes in government policy, such as those reflected in changes in bank rate; in fact, they appear to be very much affected by daily events, including movements on the stock exchanges, but the effect is on their feeling of confidence and not necessarily on their explicit assessment of the future. However, the growing belief in the stability of the economy kept fluctuations in confidence within bounds.'

Williams and Scott conducted a case study of 13 investment decisions; each case being submitted by a different member firm of The Centre for Business Research at the University of Manchester. Only 10 of the cases studied concerned 'investment' as defined in ch. 1 § 2. Williams and Scott found that the firms concerned did not have clearly defined objectives which provided clear-cut bases for investment decisions; moreover, they considered that many of the firms' actions could be

6 Barna (1962), p. 38.
7 ibid., p. 51.

inconsistent with profit maximisation. For example, in one firm 'great emphasis was given to continuity of employment, the provision of reasonable amenities and "satisfying occupations for those who have chosen to spend their career with us" and service to the community'.[8] Moreover, in those cases in which documented and quantitative evidence of the profitability of projects was required, the criteria used for assessing the projects (such as the use of undiscounted pre-tax rates of return) were often found to be unsatisfactory.

A similar study, though more extensive, was reported by Mackintosh (1963). During the mid 1950's, he conducted case studies of 36 companies, mainly engaged in manufacturing and with all or most of their establishments in and around the Birmingham area. The study was based on information obtained from a questionnaire, interviews, annual accounts and such outside sources as chairman's speeches and press comment. The topics covered included general procedure on investment decisions, replacement policy, and the effects of taxation. Both general budgeting and replacement policy seemed to vary considerably between firms, with very few firms requiring specific rates of return on investment. Some firms adopted the policy of 'earning before spending', indicating that for them recent profits are likely to be an important determinant of current investment. Investment assessment seemed to be slightly more sophisticated amongst the larger than amongst the smaller firms. A question was asked about the effects on investment of taxation through (a) the reduction of the yield and (b) the finance available. The most frequent answer on effects 'through yield' was none, either because yields were generally above some minimum requirement or were considered irrelevant. However, strong effects were indicated likely 'through finance', particularly by those firms whose development was limited by the availability of finance. Because of this latter factor, Mackintosh considered that the system of investment allowances was likely to have some effect on investment expenditure; moreover, 9 of the 36 firms appeared to have increased their investment because of the 'incentive effect' of the allowances.

Further evidence on the criteria used for evaluating investment projects was supplied by the N.E.D.C. survey, which was concerned solely with the purchase of machine tools. The survey covered 60 companies, and of these only 6 made use of the discounted cash flow method of investment appraisal—a method equivalent to that incorporated in the neoclassical theory of optimal capital accumulation and brought to the attention of British businessmen in recent years by

8 Williams and Scott (1965), p. 59.

Alfred (1964). Of the remaining companies, 41 made use of the 'pay-back' method, while 13 had no established method. The pay-back method estimates the period needed for the expected future profits from a project to reach its cost; for projects to be approved the required period must not exceed some stipulated length of time. The main dis-advantages of this method are that it ignores the profits expected after the necessary pay-back period, and that it does not discount the value of the expected future profits back to the present. It has been critically reviewed by such authors as Merrett and Sykes:[9]

'payback as commonly used must be seen as seriously defective both in the objective of reflecting the relative financial attractiveness of projects and as an indicator of use in risk assessment. . . . In particular, there are no means by which the method could be used for . . . achieving optimal rather than merely acceptable investment decisions.'

Other important conclusions resulting from the N.E.D.C. study were that the sophistication of methods of investment appraisal varies with the size of the firm, the larger ones using the more sophisticated tech-niques; and that only a small minority (3) of firms using the payback method took account of taxation and tax concessions.

Neild's study was confined to replacement policy, and the enquiry was limited to firms participating in a conference run by the Production Engineering Research Association. These came mainly from the engin-eering industry, whose replacement decisions relate largely to machine tools. A questionnaire was sent to 301 firms, of whom 133 returned them completed. The first question asked firms what was the main consideration underlying their decisions to replace machinery. Almost as many replied 'physical deterioration of existing machinery' as replied 'possible cost savings if existing machinery, still in working order, is replaced by new and better machinery'. In those cases in which estimates of cost savings were made, the most common method of investment appraisal was 'pay-back period' (68% of firms), and only 2% of firms used the discounted cash flow or equivalent methods. Only 18% of firms said they performed their calculations on a post-tax basis. Firms using the pay-back method showed a strong tendency to use 3, 5 or 10 years as the required pay-back period: a practice which Neild com-mented 'can be explained only by the choice of fashionable numbers'.[10]

Several United Kingdom studies have attempted to assess the influence of specific variables, particularly those affected by government policy, on investment decisions. Two of the earliest such studies were conducted

9 Merrett and Sykes (1966), pp. 100–101.
10 Neild (1964), p. 35.

by the Oxford Economists' Research Group; Meade and Andrews (1938) reported on the results of discussions with 37 businessmen, whilst Andrews (1940) analysed the results of 313 completed questionnaires relating to the rate of interest and the availability of money. Recently, attention has been focused on the effectiveness of tax allowances to investment, with studies being conducted by the Federation of British Industries (1957),[11] Hart and Prussman (1963), N.E.D.C. (1965), and Corner and Williams (1965).

Meade and Andrews' selection of 37 businessmen represented a wide range of industries, including financial institutions. The survey was conducted by first mailing a questionnaire to the businessmen, the replies to which were supplemented by subsequent discussion. Regarding the influence of short-term interest rates, including bank rate, on investment, Meade and Andrews reported:[12]

'There is almost universal agreement that short-term rates of interest do not directly affect investment in fixed capital. The reason usually given for this is either that the business does not borrow from the bank or else that the effect of changes in the rate is too small in comparison with the profit margin to make any difference.'

There was less agreement about the influence of the long-term rate of interest; although the majority of businessmen denied that it had a direct effect, seven suggested that it was of some importance. The survey explored the effect of profits on investment decisions by asking the questions:

'Does it ever happen that the existence of large undistributed profits induces businesses to embark on capital extensions which they would not have undertaken otherwise? Conversely does the desire to maintain dividends out of reserve during a depression, or to maintain a liquid position, sometimes act as an influence leading to the postponement of plant renewals or desirable capital extensions?'

The answer revealed a considerable divergence of business practice:[13]

'Those who asserted that the presence of liquid resources induced extensions or renewals were more numerous than those who denied this; and those who asserted that the absence of liquid resources discouraged extensions and renewals were again more numerous than those who denied this. But those two majorities are not composed of the same entrepreneurs.'

11 Reported in Principal Memoranda of Evidence to the Committee on the Working of the Monetary System, Vol. 2, pp. 118–121.
12 Meade and Andrews (1938), p. 28.
13 ibid., p. 30.

The number of firms represented in the Meade and Andrews study was necessarily limited by the method adopted—that of an intensive personal interview. Moreover, they were mainly prosperous firms in a strong financial position. The Oxford Economists' Research Group therefore decided to extend the inquiry and send a questionnaire to as large and representative a sample of British businessmen as possible. The subsequent study, undertaken by Andrews, was conducted by sending a questionnaire to 1,308 firms, 1,000 of which were a sample drawn from the Federation of British Industries' Register of British Manufacturers, whilst the remaining 308 were selected from a list of

TABLE 3.6

Oxford Economists' Research Group survey of factors affecting
expenditure on plant extensions

Factor	Number of times mentioned
Bank rate	22
Rate of discount on bills	7
The level of interest charged on bank overdrafts	33
The facility with which bank overdrafts can be obtained	38
Yield on Government securities	2
The facility with which you can raise new capital from the public	23
Total 'mentions' (by 53 firms)	125

Source: Andrews (1940), table 1, p. 44.

public companies in non-manufacturing industries. Of the firms approached, 313 completed, or attempted to complete, the questionnaire, and of these 297 supplied answers to the questions on investment in the extension of plant which were in a form suitable for analysis. The firms had been asked to indicate which, if any, of six factors 'have . . . ever affected your decision to make, or to defer making expenditure on plant extensions'? The number of times which each factor was mentioned is shown in table 3.6; of the firms supplying answers, 246 said that none of the factors listed had ever affected their investment decisions. The cost and availability of bank overdrafts seemed to be the dominant factors; there is reason to suppose that bank rate may be regarded as important only because it affects the level of interest charged on bank overdrafts, since it was mentioned independently by only five firms.

More recent evidence on the apparent unimportance of interest rates has been provided by the survey of Corner and Williams. Out of 181 replies to the question 'Has the introduction of new plant/equipment ever been abandoned or postponed during the last 7 years owing to high interest rates', only 5 said it had ever been abandoned, though 24 said it had been postponed. A similar question revealed that 11 had abandoned, and 41 postponed such investment because of 'difficulty in obtaining finance'.

In 1957, the Federation of British Industry conducted a large-scale postal survey amongst its members to obtain evidence for presentation to the Radcliffe Committee on the Working of the Monetary System. A questionnaire was sent to 7,000 manufacturing members, though the maximum possible response was about 5,000 since subsidiaries were asked not to complete it. Replies were received from 1,595 firms. Questions on the sources and supply of funds were asked with reference to the three two-year financial year periods ending in 1953, 1955 and 1957. Between 11·5 and 13·2% of the firms had raised capital by issuing fixed interest securities or equity shares; the percentages were about 20% amongst large firms (over 700 employees) and about 5% amongst small firms (up to 200 employees). The percentage of firms deterred or prevented from raising extra money because of the cost of borrowing was very small, being greatest (about 6%) in the last period. However, 37% reported that their judgement of the profitability of new investment does vary from time to time according to the prevailing rate of interest, though neither the reasons for this nor the particular rate referred to were specified. Although only about 11% of firms stated that a particularly large rise in Bank Rate (that from 3% to 4½% during January and February 1955) was a major factor in their business decisions, its effects on them were various. Of these firms, 43% said it caused them to modify their market expectations for their product, and the percentages reporting a deferment of an investment decision or substantial reduction of an investment project because (a) of its effect on costs and (b) they considered it to be a danger signal were 39% and 29% respectively. More than half (57%) of the firms said that the heavier burden of postwar taxation had led them to expect a higher gross rate of return on new investment; the most usual gross rate of return expected was about 15–20%. Questions were also asked about firms' reactions to changes in initial and investment allowances; 23% said that since 1951 their investment decisions had been materially affected by favourable changes in the allowances, and 14% said that they had been so affected by unfavourable changes.

As a contribution to National Productivity Year (1963), Hart and

Prussman conducted a postal survey amongst 400 firms in the S.E. Hants. area. The questionnaire included the question: 'Have investment allowances for plant and machinery at any time proved to be an inducement to your concern to replace (or add to) plant and machinery'? Of the 116 respondents, 42 answered the question affirmatively; larger firms doing so more frequently than smaller ones. This survey may be compared with another conducted in the same year, and reported by Corner and Williams. Their survey was confined to businesses in southwest England operating in extractive or manufacturing industries. Questionnaires were sent to 380 establishments (as distinct from businesses or firms), and a total of 210 replies were received. Out of 181 classifiable returns, 29 were found to be responsive to (either) initial or investment allowances, and 29 to both types of allowance. Amongst independent establishments (i.e. ones in which the 'establishment' is itself a 'firm'), responsiveness to the allowances seemed to vary with the size of the establishment; and growing firms were found to be more responsive than stationary or declining ones.

The N.E.D.C. survey included a question on the influence of tax concessions on investment decisions which resulted in some apparently contradictory replies. Of the 60 companies in the survey, 57 said that the tax concessions have 'no direct effect', but 16 recognised them 'as an aid to cash flow'. Of these 16, 9 said they were reasonably certain that they had resulted in their buying more machine tools than they would otherwise have done, and the other 7 considered that this might have been the case. Probably the best explanation for this apparent contradiction is that the term 'direct effect' was interpreted as relating to the profitability aspect of the tax concessions, whilst 'aid to cash flow' is obviously a reference to their liquidity aspect. The suggestion that the liquidity aspect of the allowances is more important than the profitability aspect also received tentative support from the results reported by Corner and Williams.

The evidence of these interview and questionnaire studies appears inconsistent with the business behaviour implicitly assumed in the neoclassical theories of investment. British businessmen seem to pursue objectives which may conflict with that of profit-maximisation; they have a distinct preference for internal funds, and moreover they are apparently unaccustomed to using discounting methods of investment appraisal. The majority also claim to be unaffected by the two major investment policy variables—interest rates and tax allowances.

Perhaps rather surprisingly, the results of United States studies convey an impression of similar business investment behaviour. For example, Eisner's survey notes Mack (1941) who conducted 86 personal interviews with representatives from 56 large firms in 11 different industries as seeing 'capital expenditures stimulated in large part by basic cultural values which make businessmen want to be connected with larger and more successful firms'.[14] Similarly Heller (1951) reporting an interview study of 13 manufacturing firms in the Minneapolis—St. Paul area noted that investment was inhibited by insufficient 'adoption of more scientific methods of calculating business advantage–of discovering the opportunities for cost savings, and hence profits, in replacement, improvements and modernization'.[15] Eisner further quotes Mack's finding that 'the bulk of capital expenditures are financed by retained earnings and there is a tendency to devote relatively constant proportions of earnings to dividends and capital expenditures. . . . the depreciation allowance is a major boundary in determining the volume of expenditures'.[16] Gort (1951), who interviewed executives of 25 electric utility companies, and supplemented his study with an examination of internal firm records, has described the pervasive importance of financial factors:[17]

'When a drop in earnings reduces the amount of cash available from internal sources and when external financing becomes more difficult, a strong pressure toward retrenchment develops even though the company is able to obtain funds, if necessary. It is frequently difficult to cite specific projects which have been eliminated or deferred, since these pressures manifest themselves in more subtle ways. For example, the tests applicable to the approval of capital expenditures become more rigid. Replacement and maintenance expenditures tend to be postponed even though construction costs are lower, and junior staff become less inclined to recommend improvements which may be vetoed at top management levels.'

Finally, summarising the American studies, Eisner observed that:[18]

'There are numerous reports that current interest rates have no direct connection with investment decisions. These are documented by various statements by businessmen that they never consider interest rate changes at all, or simply that such considerations never influence investment decisions.'

More recent evidence that the investment behaviour of United States firms remains relatively unsophisticated has been provided by Istvan (1961) and Pullara and Walker (1965). Istvan conducted interviews with 149 executives in 48 large companies, and found that only 7 firms employed an investment criteria that involved discounting future money

14 Eisner (1957), p. 526.
15 Heller (1951), p. 103.
16 Eisner (1957), p. 551.
17 Gort (1951), p. 187.
18 Eisner (1957), p. 563.

flows. As many as 37 of the companies employed the crude pay-back method, and its reciprocal, the simple rate of return. Both of these methods ignore the time dimension of the expected returns from the investment, and the returns received after the money value of the investment has been recouped. The findings of this study are confirmed by the subsequent questionnaire study of 150 large chemical firms conducted by Pullara and Walker. These authors concluded:[19]

'In the chemical industry, a surprisingly large proportion of firms rely on subjective judgment and are willing to admit it. Judgment, or judgment plus payback, is the overwhelmingly popular method among small and medium-sized firms and accounts for roughly half of even the large firms.'

The overwhelming impression of both the United Kingdom and the United States questionnaire surveys is therefore that actual business practice is inconsistent with the neoclassical theories of investment. In particular, interest rates seem to be of less importance and internal funds of more importance than such theories predict. The factors which businessmen—especially those reported in the American surveys—stress are those of capacity and competitive market pressures. Theories of aggregate investment centred around output changes and capital utilisation may therefore be more realistic than those centred on expected yields and the cost of funds. However the validity of this tentative conclusion is wholly dependent upon the reliability and significance of the results of interview and questionnaire studies. Both the methodology and potential usefulness of such studies have been criticised, notably by White (1956)[20] and Eisner (1957).[21]

A typical feature of interview and questionnaire studies of business behaviour is their low response rate. Amongst the recent United Kingdom studies described, the following response rates were achieved: Mackintosh, 30%; F.B.I. 32%; Barna, 43%; Hart and Prussman, 34%; Neild, 43%; and Corner and Williams, 63%. The importance of the response rate depends primarily on whether or not the firms responding are representative of those in the population. There are grounds for supposing that it is the more progressive and enlightened firms which respond to questionnaire and interview approaches; 'failure to reply may result from inertia or from inhibition if the firm's practices are felt to be backward'.[22] Questionnaires which aim to explore the significance

19 Pullura and Walker (1965), p. 406.
20 This article includes a detailed criticism of the Oxford studies, see pp. 566–577.
21 See especially pp. 513–518, and the subsequent comments by Morgan (1957), pp. 584–590.
22 Neild (1964), p. 39.

of specific variables may not be completed simply because firms fail to appreciate the potential importance of those variables. For example, although only about 25% of the respondents to Andrews' survey indicated that the cost of capital was ever a factor in their decisions to invest in either fixed capital or stocks, Sayers (1940) considered even this figure to be 'an overstatement of the general attitude of British businessmen—on the ground that practically all of the 77% of the recipients who failed to answer the questionnaire probably did so because they had been affected neither by capital cost changes nor by capital or credit rationing and therefore considered the questionnaire silly'.[23]

Even if the response rate is high, the responding firms may not be representative of all firms in the population, because the sample of firms selected for interview or questionnaire study may itself not be representative. For example, the questionnaire in Neild's study was addressed to those who attended a conference on replacement policy; 'these may well be representatives of the better firms, which are at least conscious that replacement policy matters'.[24] Another common criticism directed towards survey studies is their frequent use of an unweighted random sample of all the firms in the population. White, criticising Andrews' study, wrote:[25]

'Randomness is undesirable when the responses are not weighted, because it must cause the sample to be dominated by small firms; these are naturally much more numerous than large ones, whether for industry as a whole or within separate industries. Now the investment carried out by the average small firm must be both minor in comparison with the investment of the average large firm and also, . . . less open to the influence of changing capital costs. But since the objective of the survey was to obtain information on the responsiveness of aggregate investment to changes in capital costs, the replies ought to have been weighted in proportion to the respondents' normal (or potential) investments.'

Failure to weight replies by size of firm, or amount of investment, is only of consequence if the size of a firm is likely to affect its replies to the questions under consideration. But, as White observed:[26]

'there is strong reason for expecting the smaller firms to be less sensitive to changes in the cost of capital . . . That relatively small firms are predominantly self-financiers is indicated by the well-known difficulty which small firms have in raising capital from the public by bond and share issues. Public

23 White (1956), p. 567.
24 Neild (1964), p. 39.
25 White (1956), p. 568.
26 ibid., pp. 570–571.

unfamiliarity with the firm makes sale of its securities difficult so that, even if underwriters should be willing to sponsor an issue, the cost of the funds will be extremely high. This is especially the case for stock issues. And the inherent dangers for a small firm in the (high) fixed interest charges of a bond issue discourages use of this source of capital.'

The meaningfulness of the replies actually received from businessmen has also been queried. For example, in discussing the role of irrational or nonrational attitudes in inhibiting investment, Mack reported that:[27]

'When the point was narrowed down to specific examples, however, reasons from refraining from the venture seemed based on a perfectly reasonable judgment about business advantages. The unreasonableness lay only in the motive ascribed for the decision.'

Thus as Eisner commented:[28]

'it is clear that one cannot accept respondents' descriptions or explanations of what they do at face value without further examination. It is quite possible that the individual businessman does not really know, in any sense satisfactory to the economist, what determines his investment decisions. We may add that, if he did know he might not tell!'

Moreover, as Gort (1957) pointed out, decisions to invest are usually taken by groups of individuals within a firm, and not by a single person:[29]

'An investment decision . . . may entail negotiations, discussion, and exchange of technical memoranda, extending over many months, with some sixty or seventy officials involved in the process. It is unreasonable, therefore, to suppose that any one official will have answers to all of the questions an economist may wish to ask.'

Not only may any one individual within a firm be unable to supply all the answers, but different individuals may supply different answers to the same question; the answers differing according to the individual's role in the firm and his place in the decision-making structure. For example, a production manager who is required to justify proposed capital expenditures in terms of increased production or cost savings sufficient to realise some specified earnings criteria, is likely to identify expected profitability rather than the cost or availability of capital as

27 Mack (1941), p. 270.
28 Eisner (1957), p. 514.
29 Gort (1957), p. 594.

the principal factor affecting the investment decision. However, the firm's finance department may have previously stipulated the earnings criteria in the light of the current cost and availability of capital. Moreover the very reporting of interview studies is itself a highly subjective task and should therefore be viewed with some caution. Eisner offered the following conclusion:[30]

'The investigator conducting is by its nature a personal method of research and those fellow economists ... have every right to wonder whether they have anything more in a reporter of interviews than, at best, a good storyteller. Unfortunately there may be as many only vaguely related "stories" as there are raconteurs. "Morals" of the stories are likely to be at least as numerous.'

Even if interview and questionnaire studies successfully elicit information about the variables which individual firms consider to be the important determinants of their investment decisions, they may still not provide much guide to the variables which are important at the macro level. (See ch. 2 § 1.) In particular, individual firms are likely to underestimate the effects on aggregate investment of those variables which affect all of them in the same way, such as interest rates and tax allowances to investment. As Eisner commented:[31]

'the rate of interest is one of these variables whose effect, whatever it may be, tends to be an aggregative phenomenon and not, by its nature, a factor in which variations in experiences of one firm (such as a gain in sales at the expense of a competitor) are cancelled substantially by similar changes in an opposite direction for another firm.'

Thus 'the traditional role of the interest rate in influencing the level of investment may be quite consistent with a situation in which only 5% of firms pay any attention to the interest rate'.[32] Much of the economic theory relates to marginal considerations, and so 'the investigator must avoid what may be called a public opinion poll mentality which would decide issues of economic theory by a meaningless majority vote'.[33] The significance of particular variables in the determination of aggregate investment can only be assessed successfully by first formulating econometric models to explain the aggregate, and then subjecting them to appropriate statistical testing.

Perhaps the most serious inherent weakness in interview and ques-

30 Eisner (1957), p. 567.
31 ibid., p. 516.
32 ibid., p. 517.
33 ibid., p. 517.

tionnaire studies is that although they may be useful in testing hypotheses about human and firm behaviour, they are not readily amenable to quantitative prediction. They may successfully predict what percentage of firms, and also what proportion of aggregate investment, may be influenced by, say, future changes in tax allowances, but they cannot predict the quantitative effect of such a change on aggregative investment. Even if questions required respondents to report whether they were influenced 'never', 'a little', or 'much', predictions would be barely possible because the interpretation of such classifications is necessarily highly subjective. Quantitative prediction can only be achieved using econometric methods, which allow the past quantitative effects of different variables on investment to be measured, and then used as the basis for subsequent prediction.

However, some very important guidelines for econometric research have resulted from two questionnaire studies of the lag distributions affecting plant and equipment investment by U.S. firms conducted by Mayer. One study related particularly to war-time conditions,[34] namely those during World War II and the Korean war, and will not be reported here. The other was based on a questionnaire sent in 1954 to 276 companies in the United States who were listed in the Engineering News Record between January 1954, and January 1955, as building industrial plants, electric power plants, or plant additions.[35] Replies with usable data were received from 40% of the companies contacted and these related to 90 projects whose costs ranged from $80,000 to $300 million. The mean times between different stages in the investment process are shown in table 3.7; the means have been calculated by weighting the times for individual projects by their respective costs. Since the figures in table 3.7 are means, they obviously do not reveal the variation among individual projects, nor the form of lag distribution relevant for aggregate investment. The variations between different projects for certain important phases of the investment process are summarised in table 3.8. There appeared to be no significant difference between the lag distributions for complete plants and those for additions to existing plants, but there was a significant correlation between time and cost of plant. The longest lag in the investment process, as revealed by this survey, is that between the consideration and the construction of a project. However, Mayer did not consider this to be necessarily relevant when studying the factors, and in particular monetary policy variables, which affect investment:[36]

34 See Mayer (1953), summarised in Sonenblum and Mayer (1955).
35 Reported in Mayer (1958) and Mayer (1960).
36 Mayer (1958), pp. 362–363.

INVESTMENT: AN ECONOMIC AGGREGATE

TABLE 3.7

The timing of United States industrial plant investment
investment-weighted means

Time from	Number in months
Start of consideration to start of construction	22
Start of drawing of plans to start of construction	7
Final decision to build to start of construction	6
Placing of first significant orders to start of construction	2
Start of financing to start of construction	4
Completion of financing to start of construction	3
Start of construction to completion	15

Source: Mayer (1958), table 4, p. 364.

TABLE 3.8

Lag distribution of three stages in United States
industrial plant investment

Percentage distribution of time from start of

Drawing of plans to start of construction		Placing of first significant order to start of construction		Start of construction to completion	
Months	%	Months	%	Months	%
0	11	Negative	22	6 and below	16
1–3	29	0	32	7–9	27
4–6	29	1–3	25	10–12	37
7–9	14	4–6	16	13–15	6
10 and over	17	7 and over	5	16–18	7
				19 and over	7
	100		100		100

Source: Mayer (1960), table 2, p. 130.

'an easy money policy may cause businessmen to start considering the purchase of new plant and equipment. In this case the relevant lag is quite long, being the time from the start of consideration to the start of construction. On the other hand, an easy money policy may cause businessmen to approve projects which otherwise would have been rejected. The relevant lag, in this case, is the time between the final decision . . . and the start of construction. Finally, an easy money policy might affect investment at an even later stage by preventing the cancellation of previously approved projects. . . .

'For a tight money policy, too, there are several possibilities. Thus, at one extreme, a tight money policy can discourage the start of consideration of new projects; in this case there is a long lag until expenditures are affected. Or, to take a less extreme case, it can prevent the final approval of some previously considered projects. At the other extreme, some companies probably ignore a tight money policy until they reach the stage of trying to obtain external financing for the project, and in this case the lag is quite short. The completion of financing data is probably an extreme limit; in most cases after financing has been obtained for a project it is unlikely to be cancelled because credit is tightened.'

There are grounds for supposing that Mayer's survey sheds more light on the correct specification of aggregate investment relationships than do the other questionnaire and interview studies described. Although the response rate was low, there is no obvious reason why the investment of responding firms should have a different lag distribution from those of non-respondents, or from those of firms not included in the sample (at least for the same type of investment). Moreover, since very small projects were excluded from the survey, and the time lags relating to the others were weighted according to the costs of the projects, the results are likely to be representative of aggregate investment in industrial plant. Finally, the results do permit a quantitative prediction relating to one important aspect of the aggregate investment process, namely the shape of the investment lag distribution. The following chapter discusses the problems associated with estimating this lag function using econometric methods.

Chapter 4

ESTIMATION OF LAG DISTRIBUTIONS

4.1. Introduction

As outlined in ch. 2 § 11, any investment process is subject to a number of separate time lags, and for aggregate investment the total lag distribution is likely to be highly complex. This is primarily because of differences in the lag distributions associated with different types of capital goods, different purchasing firms and different sources of supply. Moreover the lag distribution may vary through time as the result of changes in routines of investment appraisal, production technique and the pressure of demand on the capital goods industries.

The treatment of lag distributions in regression analysis of aggregate investment has increased in sophistication throughout the years. Early studies usually either ignored the problem of lags completely, or used only one single lagged value of the explanatory variables. However in the 1950's, and particularly after the stimulus of Koyck's (1954) work on geometrically declining lag distributions, alternative ways of estimating distributed lag functions were developed and applied. But until very recently the lag distribution was always—and usually only implicitly—assumed to be stable. During the early 1960's particularly, considerable time and effort was expended on estimating stable lag distributions of increasingly complex form, when only casual inspection of ex ante and ex post investment data showed the lag distributions to be subject to considerable inter-temporal variation. Realistic allowance for the effects of changes in demand pressure on the capital goods industries was finally provided by the work of Popkin (1965, 1966) and Tinsley (1967).

This chapter attempts a brief survey and evaluation of the methods of estimating both stable and variable lag distributions; a somewhat more sophisticated survey having recently been provided by Griliches (1967). The remainder of this section deals with the basic specification of a stable lag distribution, section 2 with geometrically declining lag distributions, section 3 with Pascal and rational lag distributions, and section 4 with other methods of estimating stable lag distributions. Section 5 then examines alternative methods of allowing the lag distribution to vary through time, whilst the final section 6 presents a non-regression method of estimating the inter-temporal variations in lags.

Although any investment function which is even only approximately properly specified will have several explanatory variables, the expositions of the alternative methods have usually been with reference to the simpler case of only one explanatory variable. That is, they have been concerned with the problem of estimating equations of the form[1]

$$I_t = \beta_0 X_t + B_1 X_{t-1} + \beta_2 X_{t-2} + \ldots + u_t, \qquad (4.1)$$

where I is the dependent variable (say investment), X is a single explanatory variable, and u is a random disturbance such that

$$
\begin{aligned}
E(u_t) &= 0 && \text{for all } t, \\
E(u_t\, u_{t+j}) &= \begin{cases} 0 & \text{for } j \neq 0 \\ \sigma_n^2 & \text{for } j = 0. \end{cases} && (4.2)
\end{aligned}
$$

The coefficients β_0, β_1, β_2, etc., are assumed to have a finite sum, and usually to be all non-negative. This latter assumption implies that the effect of any particular value of X is divided up between the corresponding and successive values of I. Thus equation (4.1) can be rewritten as

$$I_t = \beta\, [w_0 X_t + w_1 X_{t-1} + w_2 X_{t-2} + \ldots] + u_t \qquad (4.3)$$

where the w_i are all non-negative and sum to unity and β measures the total effect of a change in X on I. The pattern of the w's describes the relative influence of different lagged values of X on current I; that is, the form of the distributed lag function.

Equation (4.3) could be estimated by regressing I_t on the appropriate values of X (X_t, X_{t-1}, X_{t-2}, ...); all lagged values of X whose coefficients were not specified 'a priori' as zero being included in the regression equation. However, to the extent that successive values of X are serially correlated, the different variables in the regression equation (corresponding to successive values of X) will be multicollinear, and hence the estimates of the w's will be subject to large sampling variances. By considering various examples, Alt (1942) showed that as more lagged values of X are introduced, a stage is reached when the sampling variances become so great as to render the coefficients erratic, with some

---

1 For ease of exposition, the subsequent discussion ignores the existence of any constant term in this relationship. However, the conclusions would not be materially affected if a constant term were to be included.

not even satisfying very general 'a priori' requirements. The problem is aggravated when a more realistic specification of the basic investment relationship is made by including more than just a single explanatory variable, since the relevant variables may themselves be multicollinear. Moreover, since the total number of variables to be included in the regression equation will be equal to the product of the number of different explanatory variables and the number of relevant lagged values of each,[2] the number of degrees of freedom associated with the estimation procedure is likely to be seriously reduced, thus further reducing the efficiency with which each of the separate coefficients can be estimated.

Much of the early regression analysis of aggregate investment avoided these problems, perhaps unwittingly, by specifying an investment relationship which included only one observation on each of the different explanatory variables. Some even assumed that the only relevant values of the explanatory variables are those relating to the current time period; thus all the w's other than w_0 were specified as zero. The magnitude of the error involved in making this (often implicit) assumption is dependent on the length of the unit time period. For annual data, and certain types of investment goods, the true value of w_0 may be fairly large,[3] whereas for monthly data, w_0 is likely to be very close to zero. However, use of too long a unit time period is likely to involve another type of specification error. This is because the implicit assumption that all experience of an explanatory variable within any particular unit time period has exactly the same effect on the dependent variable becomes less realistic the longer is the unit time period.

The importance of a time lag misspecification is likely to depend on the nature of the variable under consideration. For variables which are highly serially correlated (their trend predominating over other influences), the misspecification will affect the magnitude of the coefficient attached to the variable, rather than its sign or significance. However, the effects are more serious when dealing with variables which show a marked cyclical pattern. This can be seen by considering a hypothetical economy in which investment is simply a negative function of the interest rate lagged two years, and in which investment, the aggregate pressure of demand, monetary policy, and the interest rate in turn follow similar four-year cycles. Only by specifying a two-year lag

2 Assuming that the same form of lag distribution is relevant for each of the explanatory variables.

3 For annual data, and for fixed time lags of one year or less, the coefficient w_0 is given by $w_0 = (12 - \theta)/12$, where θ is the time lag in months. For fixed time lags of more than one year, w_0 is zero.

between the interest rate and investment would one obtain a true measure of the effects of the interest rate on investment; a lag misspecification of one year would reveal no correlation between the two variables; whilst a lag misspecification of two years (e.g. one in which instantaneous reaction was assumed) would yield a perfect correlation of the wrong (positive) sign. Some of the unexpected results of regression analysis, and particularly those relating to the insignificance of the interest rate, may be attributable to such an incorrect specification of the basic lag structure.

4.2. Geometrically Declining Lag Distributions

Because direct estimation of equations such as (4.3) is subject to serious problems of multicollinearity and limited degrees of freedom various authors have attempted to overcome these problems by making certain 'a priori' assumptions about the form of the lag distribution In particular, Koyck (1954) showed that by assuming the series of weights w_0, w_1, w_2 . . . declines geometrically, the basic investment equation can be reduced to one involving only two independent variables, X_t and I_{t-1}. Following this assumption, equation (4.3) can be rewritten as

$$I_t = \beta[w_0\ X_t + w_0\ \lambda X_{t-1} + w_0\ \lambda^2\ X_{t-2} + . . .] + u_t \qquad (4.4)$$

where $0 \leqslant \lambda < 1$. Lagging equation (4.4) by one period, and multiplying through by $\lambda(0 \leqslant \lambda < 1)$ yields

$$\lambda\ I_{t-1} = \beta[w_0\ \lambda\ X_{t-1} + w_0\ \lambda^2\ X_{t-2} + w_0\ \lambda^3\ X_{t-3} + . . .] + \lambda\ u_{t-1}.$$
$$(4.5)$$

Finally subtracting equation (4.5) from equation (4.4) gives

$$I_t - \lambda\ I_{t-1} = \beta\ w_0\ X_t + u_t - \lambda\ u_{t-1},$$

and hence

$$I_t = \beta\ w_0\ X_t + \lambda\ I_{t-1} + (u_t - \lambda\ u_{t-1}). \qquad (4.6)$$

Now since

$$\sum_{i=0}^{i=\infty} w_i = \sum_{i=0}^{i=\infty} w_0\ \lambda^i = \frac{w_0}{1-\lambda} = 1,$$

w_0 must equal $(1-\lambda)$. Hence, denoting $\beta\ w_0$ by α an estimate of β can be obtained by dividing the estimate of α by one minus the estimate of λ.

The realism of this formulation is again dependent on the length of the unit time period; the shorter the unit time period the less realistic is the assumption that w_0 is the largest of the w's. However, the assumption can be modified to allow a number of the first w's to be freely determined—but only at the expense of including the same number of additional variables in the final (reduced-form) equation. Thus,

$$I_t = \beta[w_0 \, X_t + w_1 \, X_{t-1} + w_2 \, X_{t-2} + w_2 \, \lambda \, X_{t-3} + w_2 \, \lambda^2 \, X_{t-4} + \ldots] + u_t \tag{4.7}$$

reduces to

$$I_t = \beta \, w_0 \, X_t + (w_1 - w_0 \, \lambda) \, X_{t-1} + (w_2 - w_1 \, \lambda) \, X_{t-2} + (u_t - \lambda \, u_{t-1}). \tag{4.8}$$

This flexibility allows different lag distributions for the different explanatory variables, although the weights of each eventually follow the same geometrically declining pattern (i.e. λ is unique to the relationship and not to individual explanatory variables).

Although equations of the form of (4.6), (4.8) provide an escape from the statistical problems of multicollinearity and limited degrees of freedom, their estimation is subject to other difficulties.[4] Since economic variables are usually highly serially correlated, a regression of I_t on I_{t-1} and any (or no) other variables is likely to yield a good overall fit, and a significant positive coefficient for I_{t-1}, irrespective of the explanatory variables (and the lag distribution of their weights) which actually determine I_t. The interpretation of estimated regression equations of this form is therefore fraught with difficulty. Moreover, equations which include a lagged value of the dependent variable invalidate one of the basic assumptions of linear regression analysis since, in such formulations, the error term is not independent of subsequent values of the lagged dependent variable.[5] The consequence is that the least-squares estimates will be biased, though if the disturbance term follows a normal distribution, they will tend to have the desirable asymptotic properties of consistency and efficiency. This means that as the sample size (the number of observations) increases, the expected value of the bias tends to zero, and that of all estimators with this property, least-squares is the one that provides estimates with the smallest variance. Unfortunately, the number of observations in time series analysis is usually strictly limited, both by the availability of consistent and reliable data and by the necessity of assuming that the structure of the relationship remained constant throughout the time period under study. Thus the fact that

4 The following discussion of these difficulties, and the proposed methods of overcoming them, owes much to Johnston (1963), pp. 211–221; to ch. 10 of Johnston (forthcoming), and to Malinvaud (1966), pp. 467–472.

5 It can be seen from equation (4.6) that since the error term $(u_t - \lambda u_{t-1})$ influences I_t it is not independent of the lagged dependent variable I_t in the equation for I_{t+1}.

estimates may have desirable large sample properties is of little consolation if their small sample properties are clearly unsatisfactory.
Further, the estimation of equations of the form of (4.6), (4.8) is compli-
cated by the fact that when they are estimated using time-series data,
the error terms $(u_t - \lambda u_{t-1})$ will be autocorrelated even if the original
error terms u_t are serially independent. Only if u follows the first-order
Markov scheme

$$u_t - \lambda u_{t-1} = \varepsilon_t \qquad (4.9)$$

where ε is assumed to have the error term properties of equations (4.2),
will $(u_t - \lambda u_{t-1})$ be serially independent. Unless this is the case, the joint
occurrence of lagged variables and autocorrelated error terms has the
consequence that the least squares estimate will be not only biased, but
also inconsistent. Griliches (1961) has derived expressions for the
asymptotic bias in the ordinary least squares estimates, and Orcutt and
Cochrane (1949) have shown that the biases produced in finite sample
sizes can be very serious.

Moreover the problem is even further aggravated by the fact that
the econometrician may not realise that the errors are autocorrelated,
since the conventional Durbin–Watson test for autocorrelation will be
biased towards the values consistent with serially independent errors.
On the other hand, the problems may become quantitatively less serious
as further exogenous variables are introduced into equations like (4.6),
(4.8). Malinvaud (1966), following the exposition of Griliches (1961),
has shown[6] that the effect of introducing an exogenous variable such
as X_t into an equation of the form

$$I_t = \lambda I_{t-1} + u_t - \lambda u_{t-1} \qquad (4.10)$$

is to reduce the asymptotic bias in the estimate of λ. Secondly, another
test for autocorrelation, which is applicable when lagged dependent
variables are present, has recently been developed by Durbin; however
the test is appropriate only for large samples, nothing yet being known
about its small sample properties.

Despite these consolations, the joint effects of lagged variables and
autocorrelation on the least squares estimates of the parameters of
equations such as (4.6) are so serious that alternative methods of estimation have been devised.[7]

6 Malinvaud (1966), pp. 459–465.

7 The remainder of this section discusses these alternative methods. It may prove
too difficult for those acquainted with only the elements of regression analysis.
Moreover as it concerns a topic subject to much recent and current enquiry, it may
quickly become out-dated by subsequent publications.

These methods relate to one or other of four possible situations. Identifying the error term in equation (4.6), $u_t - \lambda u_{t-1}$ by v_t, these can be distinguished as:[8]

(i) The u's are serially independent, and λ is known.
(ii) The u's are serially independent, but λ is unknown.
(iii) Neither the u's nor the v's are serially independent, but the serial dependence of the v's is known.
(iv) Neither the u's nor the v's are serially independent, and the serial dependence of the v's is unknown.[9]

Given that one of the reasons for estimating equations such as (4.6) is to determine the form of the lag distribution, it is highly unlikely that the value of λ is known. Moreover, since the geometrically declining lag distribution assumed in equation (4.4) can at best only be an approximation to the true form of the lag distribution, it is probably somewhat misspecified, and thus the u's are unlikely to be serially independent. It would be surprising if the nature of this serial dependence were known, or could even be guessed. Thus the ranking of the four situations by their relative frequency of occurrence may well be (iv), (ii), (iii) and (i). Unfortunately the more likely situations happen to be those for which the problems of estimation are greatest.

8 A rather similar classification was made with reference to a consumption function by Zellner and Geisel (1968), who showed that the estimates of the basic relationship under study (in this case α and λ) are sensitive to what is assumed about the properties of the error terms. They also showed how a Bayesian approach, incorporating both prior and sample information, can be used to discriminate between alternative assumptions on the basis of their posterior probabilities.

9 Note that since $v_t = u_t - \lambda u_{t-1}$, knowledge of the serial dependence of the u's implies knowledge of the serial dependence of the v's.
If, for example $u_t = \rho u_{t-1} + \eta_t$
then $\lambda u_{t-1} = \rho \lambda u_{t-2} + \rho \eta_{t-1}$
and $v_t = \rho v_{t-1} + (\eta_t - \rho \eta_{t-1})$
Alternatively if $v_t = \rho v_{t-1} + \eta_t$
then $u_t - \lambda u_{t-1} = \rho(u_{t-1} - \lambda u_{t-2}) + \eta_t$
and $u_t = (\rho + \lambda) u_{t-1} - \rho \lambda u_{t-2} + \eta_t$
The second of these alternatives is chosen for treatment in the discussion of situations (iii) and (iv). This choice has been governed purely by virtue of its expositional and computational simplicity as compared with the first alternative. The first alternative has been considered by Koyck (1954), Klein (1958), Malinvaud (1961), and Zellner and Geisel (1968). Koyck suggested a method similar to that discussed under situation (ii) but with ρ specified to assume various values other than zero, and with alternative estimates of α and λ being obtained for each of these values of ρ. For each value of ρ, these estimates would be consistent, and Koyck's empirical studies revealed little variation in these estimates over a wide range of ρ values. As an alternative, Klein proposed an iterative method, but Malinvaud subsequently showed that the resulting estimates are not consistent. Zellner and Geisel used a method very similar to the one discussed under situation (ii).

In situation (i), equation (4.6), can be written as

$$I_t = \alpha X_t + \lambda I_{t-1} + (u_t - \lambda u_{t-1}) \qquad (4.11)$$

or

$$I_t = \alpha X_t + \lambda I_{t-1} + v_t \qquad (4.12)$$

or

$$I_t - \lambda I_{t-1} = \alpha X_t + (u_t - \lambda u_{t-1}) \qquad (4.13)$$

where λ is known. By regressing $(I_t - \lambda I_{t-1})$ on X_t as in equation (4.13) no lagged variable appears on the right-hand side, and the estimation problems are simply those associated with the autocorrelated errors. The method of generalised least-squares[10] may then be applied to obtain a best linear unbiased estimate of α.

Situation (ii) has been examined by Koyck (1954) and Klein (1958), who have derived different but equivalent methods for obtaining consistent estimates of α and λ. Koyck's method involves two stages: the first is to regress I_t on X_t and I_{t-1}, and compute the sum of squared residuals; the second is to solve two simultaneous equations, one of which incorporates this sum, to yield estimates of α and λ. In Klein's method, equation (4.11) is first rewritten as

$$(I_t - u_t) = \alpha X_t + \lambda(I_{t-1} - u_{t-1}) \qquad (4.14)$$

which is then estimated as an 'errors-in-variables' problem.[11] Since $E(u_t^2) = E(u_{t-1}^2)$, the two variables I_t and I_{t-1} are assumed to be measured with the same error variance, and X_t without error. Although the estimates obtained by these methods are consistent, they are still biased. Recently, Zellner and Geisel (1968) have proposed a method which may yield estimates of the parameters that possess the usual ordinary least-squares properties of consistency, unbiasedness and efficiency. Their method involves a transformation of equation (4.11) such that the elements in the data matrix become functions of λ and the observed X-values. Alternative values of λ are then assumed, and for each the application of ordinary least squares yields estimates of the other parameters which possess the usual O-L-S properties. The final estimate of λ, and hence of the other parameters, is chosen as being that which minimises the sum of squared residuals.

The errors in equations (4.11, 12) will be serially dependent unless

$$u_t - \lambda u_{t-1} = \varepsilon_t \qquad (4.9)$$

where both u and ε have the error term properties of equation (4.2).

10 A description of this method is given in Johnston (1963), pp. 179–192.
11 A survey and bibliography of methods of dealing with the 'errors-in-variables' problem has been provided by Madansky (1959).

Suppose that the serial dependence of the v's is of the first-order Markov scheme

$$v_t = \rho\, v_{t-1} + \eta_t \qquad (4.15)$$

where η has the error term properties of (4.2). If ρ is known, the case is a simple example of situation (iii); if ρ is unknown, it is a simple example of situation (iv). Knowledge of ρ allows equation (4.12) to be combined with equation (4.15) to give

$$(I_t - \rho I_{t-1}) = \alpha(X_t - \rho X_{t-1}) + \lambda(I_{t-1} - \rho I_{t-2}) + \eta_t, \qquad (4.16)$$

which can then be estimated using ordinary least-squares. Since equation (4.16) contains a lagged variable, but a serially independent error term, the resulting estimates are biased, but consistent. This procedure can be shown to be approximately equivalent to applying generalised least-squares to the estimation of equation (4.12).[12] In the absence of any specific information about ρ, Cochrane and Orcutt (1949) recommended taking first differences of all observations before applying ordinary least squares. This procedure is equivalent to assuming that $\rho = 1$. Unfortunately a recent article by Kadiyala (1968) has shown that the efficiency of the estimator so obtained may actually be less than that of the simple least squares estimator.

Two alternative procedures are available for use in situation (iv). These are:

  (i) assume that the serial dependence of the errors is of a simple form (e.g. as in equation (4.15)) and estimate its parameters jointly with those of equation (4.12);
  (ii) use instrumental variables.

Combining equations (4.12) and (4.15), and substituting for V_{t-1} gives

$$I_t = \alpha\, X_t - \alpha\rho\, X_{t-1} + (\lambda+\rho)\, I_{t-1} - \lambda\rho\, I_{t-2} + \eta_t \qquad (4.17)$$

This equation can be estimated using ordinary least squares to give consistent, but biased, estimates of α, $\alpha\rho$, $\lambda+\rho$, and $\lambda\rho$. Unfortunately these estimates do not yield unique estimates of λ and ρ, and hence of the form of the lag distribution. An alternative approach is to use search or iterative procedures. Denoting a provisional estimate of ρ by $\hat{\rho}$, equation (4.17) may be written as

$$(I_t - \hat{\rho} I_{t-1}) = \alpha(X_t - \hat{\rho} X_{t-1}) + \lambda(I_{t-1} - \hat{\rho} I_{t-2}) + \eta_t. \qquad (4.18)$$

Provisional estimates of ρ in the range $-1 \leq \hat{\rho} \leq 1$ may be chosen, and the one which minimises the sum of squared residuals, and the

12 See Johnston (1963), pp. 186–187.

associated estimates of α and λ, chosen as the final estimates. Alternatively a single value of $\hat{\rho}$ may be specified, and used to obtain estimates of α and λ by fitting equation (4.18), which in turn may be substituted into

$$I_t - \lambda I_{t-1} - \alpha X_t = \rho(I_{t-1} - \lambda I_{t-2} - \alpha X_{t-1}) + \eta_t \qquad (4.19)$$

to give a new estimate for ρ. (Equation (4.19) is simply a reformulation of equation (4.17).) This secondary estimate of ρ can then be used to obtain secondary estimates of α and λ, and the procedure continued until the estimates of ρ, α and λ achieve some previously specified degree of convergence. Some econometricians have combined the search and iterative procedures; using the search procedure on a wide range of values of ρ, and then taking the one which minimises the sum of squared residuals as the starting point for the iterative procedure.[13] Unfortunately search and iterative procedures are computationally expensive, and alternative procedures which yield estimates with the same asymptotic properties of consistency and efficiency have been proposed. For example, Malinvaud (1966) outlined a two-step method which involves fitting equation (4.17) using ordinary least squares, and then estimating ρ by

$$\hat{\rho} = -\frac{\text{coefficient of } X_{t-1}}{\text{coefficient of } X_t}$$

This estimate is substituted into equation (4.18), which can then be fitted to give estimates of α and λ.

Another approach, suggested by Taylor and Wilson (1964), is that of three-pass least squares. Combining equations (4.12) and (4.15) directly yields

$$I_t = \alpha X_t + \lambda I_{t-1} + \rho v_{t-1} + \eta_t. \qquad (4.20)$$

Their suggested estimation procedure is as follows.[14] First, equation (4.12) is estimated by least squares ignoring the autocorrelated error term. If X_t is non-autocorrelated, this gives a consistent estimate of α. The residuals from this equation are biased estimates of the true error term v_t, with the bias asymptotically proportional to I_{t-1}. These residuals are lagged one period and substituted into equation (4.20) for v_{t-1} with compensation being made for the bias by introducing I_{t-2} into the equation as well. In the second pass, equation (4.20) is estimated with $I_t - \hat{\alpha} X_t$ as the dependent variable, where $\hat{\alpha}$ is the consistent estimate of α from the first pass. This gives a consistent estimate of λ. This

---

13 For an application of such an estimation, together with a proof that the iterative procedure does converge, see Sargan (1964).

14 This description is exactly that given by Taylor and Wilson (1964), pp. 330–331, but with appropriate modification of symbols and equation numbers.

estimate of λ and the earlier estimate of α from pass one are used in equation (4.13) to obtain a consistent estimate of v_t. In the third pass, these estimates are lagged one period and substituted for u_{t-1} in equation (4.20). Finally, equation (4.20) is estimated directly by least squares to obtain consistent estimates of all the coefficients. The major weakness of this method is that in time-series studies the successive values of exogenous variables, rather than being random, are usually highly serially dependent. However, Taylor and Wilson made allowance for this fact in some Monte Carlo experiments, and still found that (for most experiments) the biases in the three-pass estimates were slight compared to those in the ordinary least squares estimates.

Two important problems remain concerning these methods of jointly estimating the serial dependence and the basic distributed lag relationship. They are (i) considerable asymptotic bias may remain if the form of the serial dependence of the residuals is incorrectly specified; and (ii) the properties of these estimation methods appear much less favourable in small as opposed to large samples. The method of instrumental variables[15] attempts to overcome the problem associated with the non-independence of I_{t-1} and v_t in equation (4.12) by first regressing I_{t-1} on some other variable(s), called 'instrumental variables', which are presumed to be independent of v_t. The resulting predicted values of I_{t-1}, namely $\hat{I}_{t-1}$, are then substituted into equation (4.12) and this is fitted using ordinary least squares to yield biased and inefficient but consistent parameter estimates. For estimating equations like (4.12), Liviatan (1963) has suggested using X_{t-1}, or even further lagged values of X, as instrumental variables. His method has been investigated by Hannan (1965), who suggested a modification of it using spectral analysis techniques to yield consistent and efficient parameter estimates. The bias in Liviatan's method has recently been derived by Nagar and Gupta (1968).

A method incorporating the instrumental variables approach and generalised least squares is due to Wallis (1967). The first step is to use X_{t-1} as an instrumental variable, regress I_t on X_t and X_{t-1}, and calculate a consistent (and unbiased) estimate of ρ from the residuals of this equation. Given this estimate of ρ, generalised least squares can be applied to yield biased, but consistent, estimates of the parameters of equation (4.12). However, given the limited number of observations usually available in time-series data, consistency may be only a small consolation. Wallis therefore conducted Monte Carlo experiments which

15 For a general exposition of the method of instrumental variables see Durbin (1958).

showed that his estimation method is superior to those of ordinary least squares, three-pass least squares, and instrumental variables in that the parameter estimates were less biased 'on the average' and showed smaller sampling variation.

4.3. Pascal and Rational Distributions

The Koyck distributed lag scheme, involving weights which decline according to a geometric progression, has been generalised by Solow (1960) and Jorgenson (1966). The Koyck formulation of equation (4.4) specifies that

$$w_i = w_0 \, \lambda^i,$$

and since

$$w_0 = (1-\lambda),$$
$$w_i = (1-\lambda) \, \lambda^i,$$

where

$$0 \leqslant \lambda < 1$$

and

$$0 \leqslant i \leqslant \infty.$$

A major criticism of this lag distribution is that the weights must always be decreasing, and do not first rise to a peak before beginning to increase. Adoption of a variant such as equation (4.7) only allows this at the cost of including more variables in the final equation to be estimated.

To discuss the generalisation of the Koyck distribution, it is helpful to use the notation of a generating function for the sequence of weights $w_0, w_1, w_2 \ldots$ Using a dummy variable Z, the polynomial function

$$A(Z) = a_0 + a_1 Z + a_2 Z^2 + a_3 Z^3 + \ldots \tag{4.21}$$

may be defined. If this function converges in some interval $-Z_0 < Z < Z_0$, then $A(Z)$ is called the generating function of the sequence $a_0, a_1, a_2, a_3 \ldots$ Moreover, if the a's are all non-negative, and sum to unity, then $A(Z)$ is a probability generating function. For example, the generating function of the w's in the Koyck distribution is given by

$$W(Z) = (1-\lambda) (1 + \lambda Z + \lambda^2 Z^2 + \lambda^3 Z^3 + \ldots) \tag{4.22}$$

$$= \frac{(1-\lambda)}{(1-\lambda Z)} \tag{4.23}$$

Solow's contribution was to consider the estimation of Pascal distributions—the convolutions of successive individual geometric distributions. The relevance of these distributions has been neatly summarised by Griliches:[16]

16 Griliches (1967), p. 20.

'We may often want to consider the effect of passing a variable (signal) through a series (cascade) of lag distributions. Thus, for example, in studying the lag between investment in research and improvements in productivity, we can think of it as the result of several lags—the lag between the investment of funds and the time inventions actually begin to appear, the lag between the invention of an idea or a device and its development up to a commercially applicable stage, and the lag which is introduced by the process of diffusion: it takes time before all the old machines are replaced by the better new ones. In each of these cases, the lag is not a fixed lag but some distribution. The form of the total lag between R and D investment and the growth in average productivity is given by a convolution of the individual lag distributions.'

Clearly the lag distribution associated with this process of innovation closely resembles that associated with the general process of investment as described in ch. 2 § 11. For example, as described in ch. 2 § 8, a firm's expectations about the future may be determined by a geometrically declining weighted spectrum of its recent experiences. Similarly the aggregate flow of expenditures resulting from decisions to invest may follow the geometric pattern. Expenditure in the first period may be relatively high since it will include not only the first progress payments due on some capital goods built to order, but also the payment for capital goods—such as vehicles—which can be bought from stock. From this period onwards, the flow of payments due for both work in progress and delivery may be expected to tail off gradually, and the pattern of the decline may be approximately geometric.

The convolution of r separate and independent lag distributions, each generated by functions $W_1(Z)$, $W_2(Z)$ . . . $W_2(Z)$, results in a total lag distribution given by

$$W_T(Z) = \frac{(1-\lambda)^r}{(1-\lambda Z)^r} = \frac{\sum_{i=0}^{i=r} (-\lambda)^i \, {}^rC_i}{\sum_{i=0}^{i=r} (-\lambda Z)^i \, {}^rC_i} \qquad (4.25)$$

which is an rth-order Pascal distribution. The advantage of assuming that the weights follow a Pascal, as opposed to a Koyck, distribution is that the former allows a much greater variety of patterns for the lag distribution. Both the mean and the variance of the Pascal distribution are functions of both r and λ. Perhaps most importantly the modal weight need not be the first: the mode occurs for i equal to the integral part of $(r\lambda-1)/(1-\lambda)$.[17] The mode is always less than the mean, and hence the distribution is skewed to the right, the skewness becoming greater as λ increases or r decreases. Pascal and Koyck distributions

17 If $(r\lambda-1)/(1-\lambda)$ is an integer, there is a double mode at $(r\lambda-1)/(1-\lambda)$ and $(r\lambda-\lambda)/(1-\lambda)$.

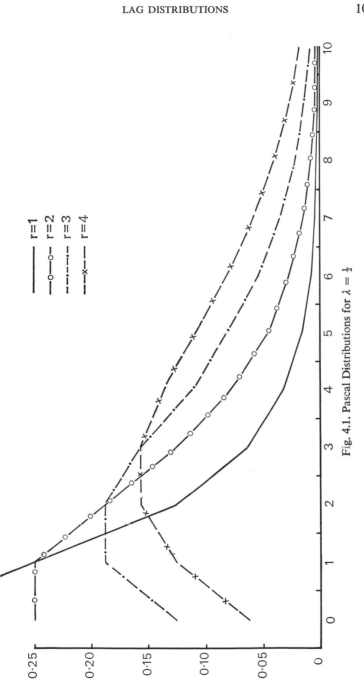

Fig. 4.1. Pascal Distributions for $\lambda = \frac{1}{2}$

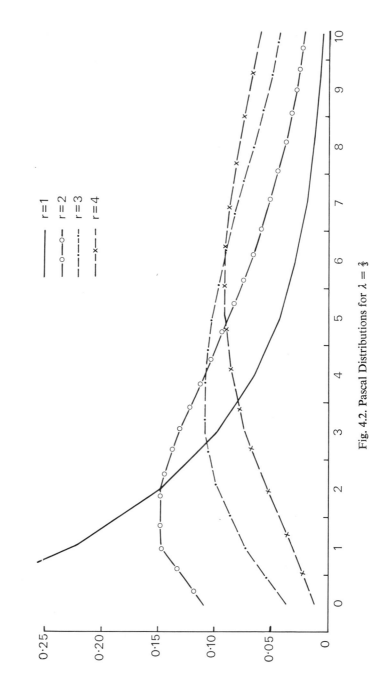

Fig. 4.2. Pascal Distributions for $\lambda = \frac{2}{3}$

for $\lambda = \frac{1}{2}$ and $\lambda = \frac{2}{3}$ are shown in figs. 4.1 and 4.2 respectively. Assuming that the weights in equation (4.3) follow an rth-order Pascal distribution, each of them is given by

$$w_i = {}^{r+i-1}C_i \, (1-\lambda)^r \, \lambda^i \qquad (4.26)$$

and the equation becomes

$$I_t = \beta(1-\lambda)^r \sum_{i=0}^{i=\infty} {}^{r+i-1}C_i \lambda^i X_{t-i} + u_t. \qquad (4.27)$$

The Koyck distributed lag form, expressed in equation (4.4) where $w_0 = (1-\lambda)$, corresponds to the special case of equation (4.27) for $r = 1$. For other values of r, estimation of equation (4.27) only becomes practicable after applying a transformation similar to that employed by Koyck. This is most conveniently explained by making use of the lag operator L, defined such that

$$L \, X_t = X_{t-1}, \, L^2 \, X_t = X_{t-2}, \text{ and } L^k \, X_t = X_{t-k}.$$

By the binomial theorem, or by repeated differentiation of the geometric series,

$$\sum_{i=0}^{i=\infty} {}^{r+i-1}C_i \, \lambda^i \, L^i = (1-\lambda L)^{-r} \qquad (4.28)$$

and hence equation (4.27) can be rewritten as

$$I_t = \beta(1-\lambda)^r \sum_{i=0}^{i=\infty} {}^{r+i-1}C_i \, \lambda^i \, L^i \, X_t + u_t. \qquad (4.29)$$

$$= \beta(1-\lambda)^r \, (1-\lambda L)^{-r} \, X_t + u_t.$$

Therefore

$$(1-\lambda)^r \, I_t = \beta(1-\lambda)^r \, X_t + (1-\lambda L)^r \, u_t \qquad (4.30)$$

or

$$I_t - {}^rC_i \, \lambda I_{t-1} + {}^rC_2 \, \lambda^2 \, I_{t-2} - \ldots + (-1)^r \, \lambda^r \, I_{t-r}$$
$$= \beta(1-\lambda)^r \, X_t + \sum_{k=0}^{k=r} {}^rC_k \, (-\lambda)^k \, u_{t-k}. \qquad (4.31)$$

There are three problems associated with the estimation of equation (4.31): (i) the strongly nonlinear way in which r enters; (ii) the nonlinear way in which λ enters; (iii) the problem of autocorrelation in the residuals. With regard to (i), Solow suggested estimating λ and β for each of several successive values of r, and choosing that value of r, and the associated estimates of λ and β, that minimises the sum of squared residuals. He also pointed out that since the expression to be minimised is a convex function of the λ_k, and the constraints define convex functions in the interval $0 \leqslant \lambda_1 \leqslant 1$, the minimisation problem might be tackled by using methods for concave programming. The problem associated with autocorrelated errors have already been discussed.

Jorgenson defined his contribution as being to 'introduce a class of distributed lag functions that has the properties that an arbitrary distributed lag function may be approximated to any desired degree of accuracy by a member of this class and that the number of parameters required for a satisfactory approximation is less than that required for an equally good approximation by a finite distributed lag function'.[18] This class is that of rational distributed lag functions: a distributed lag function is a member of this class if, and only if, its weights may be generated by the ratio of two generating functions of finite degree. Assuming that this is the case for the lag distribution of equation (4.3), that equation may be expressed as

$$I_t - u_t = \beta \ W(L) \ X_t = \beta \cdot \frac{A(L)}{B(L)} \ X_t \qquad (4.32)$$

where $A(L)$ and $B(L)$ are polynomials in the lag operator, having no characteristic roots in common, and $B(L)$ is defined such that its first term b_0 is normalised at unity. Multiplying both sides of equation (4.32) by $B(L)$ gives

$$B(L) \ [I_t - u_t] = \beta \cdot A(L) \ X_t. \qquad (4.33)$$

Hence

$$(1 + b_1 L + b_2 L^2 + \ldots + b_n L^n) \ [I_t - u_t] \\ = \beta \ (a_0 + a_1 L + a_2 L^2 + \ldots + a_m L \ ) \ X_t, \qquad (4.34)$$

and the rational distributed lag functions may be written as

$$I_t - u_t + b_1 \ (I_{t-1} - u_{t-1}) + b_2 \ (I_{t-2} - u_{t-2}) + \ldots + b_n \ (I_{t-n} - u_{t-n}) \\ = \beta \ (a_0 \ X_t + a_1 \ X_{t-1} + a_2 \ X_{t-2} + \ldots + a_m \ X_{t-m}) \qquad (4.35)$$

or

$$I_t = \beta (a_0 X_t + a_1 X_{t-1} + a_2 X_{t-2} + \ldots + a_m X_{t-m}) - b_1 I_{t-1} - b_2 I_{t-2} - \ldots \\ - b_n I_{t-n} + (u_t + b_1 u_{t-1} + b_2 u_{t-2} + \ldots + b_n u_{t-n}). \qquad (4.36)$$

It is interesting that both the Koyck and the Pascal distributed lag functions are special cases of equation (4.33) and hence of equations (4.34, 35, 36). For the Koyck function, $A(L) = 1 - \lambda$ and $B(L) = 1 - \lambda L$; and for the Pascal function, $A(L) = (1 - \lambda)^r$ and $B(L) = (1 - \lambda L)^r$.

The composite error term of equation (4.36) is both autocorrelated and correlated with each of the lagged dependent variables. The application of ordinary least squares would therefore yield biased and inconsistent parameter estimates. Jorgenson suggested estimating the parameters of equation (4.36) by applying weighted least squares, the least squares estimates being obtained as the solution of a characteristic value

18 Jorgenson (1966), p. 136.

problem. Equation (4.36) can be viewed as a generalisation of equation (4.11), since in both equations the lag distributions of I and u values are identical; and the method described by Jorgenson is a generalisation of that suggested by Koyck. Koyck's method was originally interpreted as an application of weighted least squares by Klein (1958). However, Jorgenson also showed that any distributed lag function can be approximated to any desired degree of accuracy by a rational distributed lag function of the form

$$W(L) = \frac{A_m(L)}{B_m(L)}$$

where

$$B_m(L) = \sum_{j=1}^{j=m} (S_j - L) \qquad (4.37)$$

and

$$S_j = e^j \, (j = 1 \ldots m).$$

Given some 'a priori' assumption about $B_m(L)$, Jorgenson showed how best linear unbiased estimates of the remaining parameters of equation (4.36) may be obtained. The mechanism by which estimates of the parameters of equation (4.36), that is of the coefficients of $A(L)$ and $B(L)$, are translated into estimates of the coefficients of $W(L)$ has been neatly described by Griliches (1967), using a second order case as a simple example.[19]

Although the methods developed by Solow and Jorgenson permit more flexible forms of lag distributions than the simple Koyck form, they do so only at the cost of adding more variables to the right-hand side of the final equation to be estimated. Moreover, for both methods, the final equation is almost certain to include autocorrelated errors as well as lagged variables. The estimation problems are therefore substantial, and those associated with multicollinearity are likely to grow as the number of different explanatory variables included in the basic relationship is increased. Unfortunately neither method readily permits the effects of different variables to be subject to different lag distributions, since too many variables would appear on the right-hand side of the equation to be estimated.

Perhaps the most important and disturbing criticism of estimation methods which, like those of Solow and Jorgenson, involve fitting equations which include two or more lagged (dependent) variables on the right-hand side has been made by Griliches and Wallace (1965), and

19 See Griliches (1967), pp. 23–24.

elaborated in Griliches (1967). After comparing a quarterly investment function for total U.S. manufacturing, 1948–1962, fitted by them to one fitted by Jorgenson for the same period, Griliches and Wallace concluded:[20]

> 'The substantially different distributed lag pattern implied by two rather similar equations is perhaps the most interesting finding to emerge from this comparison. It throws doubt on the whole procedure of trying to determine the shape or form of the underlying distributed lag scheme by fitting second or higher order difference equations. Small differences in the estimated coefficients have very little effect on the fit of the equation but can change drastically the implied distributed lag pattern.'

This point was demonstrated subsequently, and in a very striking manner, by Griliches in his survey article. He selected for consideration one of the better fitting equations ($R^2 = 0 \cdot 928$), from his joint study with Wallace:

$$I_t = f(X_1, X_2, X_3) + 1 \cdot 150 \, I_{t-1} - 0 \cdot 331 \, I_{t-2},$$
$$\quad\quad\quad\quad (0 \cdot 117) \quad\quad (0 \cdot 110)$$

where I_t, X_1, X_2 and X_3 are net investment, a stock price index (lagged two quarters), interest rate (industrial bonds, lagged two quarters), and capital stock respectively. The coefficients of all the explanatory variables were statistically significant and of the 'right' sign; for the lagged dependent variables, the 't' statistics are about 10 and 3 respectively. But if one constructs the 95% confidence region for the coefficients of I_{t-1} and I_{t-2}, considered simultaneously,[21] this region implies a very wide range of possible lag distributions. Three such distributions, together with that implied by the estimated equation are presented in fig. 4.3.

4.4. Other Stable Lag Distributions

Other forms of lag distribution may also be appropriate for approximating the time pattern of the aggregate investment process. One such is that of arithmetically declining weights, as presented by Fisher (1937) who described a search method of estimation.[22] His exposition related

---

20 Griliches and Wallace (1965), pp. 323–324.

21 It is illegitimate to construct 95% confidence intervals for the two coefficients independently of one another. For a description of methods of constructing joint confidence intervals see Goldberger (1964).

22 Fisher had earlier used a logarithmically normal distribution for studying the effects of price changes on the volume of trade for the U.S. economy: see Fisher (1925).

to the simple case in which $w_0 = 0$, w_1 is the modal weight, and $w_2 \ldots w_n$ taper off in an arithmetic progression. However, as Fisher observed, the method may be generalised by allowing the modal weights to be located

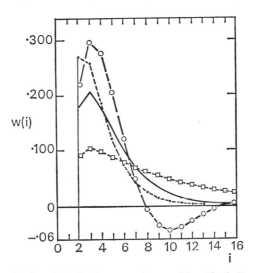

Fig. 4.3. Alternative Lag Distributions consistent with a Single Equation estimated by Griliches and Wallace (1965)

Estimated equation was
$$I = f(X_1, X_2, X_3) + 1 \cdot 150 \, I_{t-1} - 0 \cdot 331 \, I_{t-2},$$
$$(0 \cdot 12) \qquad (0 \cdot 11)$$

The lag distributions presented in the fig. correspond to coefficient of

	I_t	I_{t-1}
——————————	1·15	−0·33
—o—o—	1·35	−0·57
—·——·——·—	0·96	−0·23
—▫——▫——▫—	1·15	−0·24

elsewhere in time. The first step in the method is to specify alternative values of n, for each of which the weights are given by

$$w_1 = \frac{2n}{n(n+1)}, \quad w_2 = \frac{2(n-1)}{n(n+1)}, \quad \ldots, \quad w_n = \frac{2}{n(n+1)}. \quad (4.38)$$

These are then multiplied in turn by the corresponding lagged values of X to yield alternative total 'cause' variables. The lag distribution is chosen as being that which maximises the correlation between I_t and the total 'cause' variable, or in other words minimises the sum of squared residuals. Results obtained by using both Fisher's and Koyck's

methods have been compared, in a study of the price-elasticity of Indian
imports of British glass, by Berger (1953). He found that whilst the two
methods gave somewhat different estimates of the short-run elasticities
and the average lag, they gave identical estimates of the long-run elasticities. Choice of lag distribution, within certain limits, may therefore
not be of vital importance, especially if interest is centred on the total
effect of a variable, rather than on its distribution through time.

One particular generalisation of Fisher's assumption about the form
of the lag distribution is the inverted-V distribution. In this distribution
the weights increase at an even rate to a peak before decreasing at the
same even rate; the distribution is therefore symmetrical about its peak.
Together with the rectangular[23] and geometrically declining lag distributions, it has been used by de Leeuw in an attempt to describe the lag
distribution between actual investment expenditures and the placing
of orders relating to them. Denoting investment by I, and new orders
(net of cancellations) by N, he expressed I_t as a function of previous
new orders:

$$I_t = \sum_{i=1}^{i=n} w_i N_{t-i} \qquad (4.39)$$

where

$$\sum_{i=1}^{i=n} w_i = 1, \text{ (since orders are defined net of cancellations),}$$

and $n = $ maximum lag between order and expenditure. For the geo-
metric distribution, $w_i = (1-\lambda)\,\lambda^{i-1}$, $1 \leqslant i \leqslant \infty$; for the rectangular
distributions, $w_i = 1/n$, for $1 \leqslant i \leqslant n$; and for the inverted-V distribution, w_i (for even values of n) is given by[24]

$$w_i = \frac{4i}{n^2+2n} \text{ for } 1 \leqslant i \leqslant \frac{n}{2}, \quad w_i = \frac{4(n+1-i)}{n^2+2n} \text{ for } \frac{n}{2} \leqslant i \leqslant n,$$
$$w_i = 0 \text{ for } i > n.$$

For each of these alternatives, de Leeuw was able to reduce his basic
investment relationship to an equation fairly convenient for estimation
purposes. For the rectangular and inverted-V distributions, alternative
values of n were specified; the one that minimised the sum of squared
residuals being selected as the most appropriate. Each of the reduced
form equations contained an error term which would be autocorrelated
if the error term in the basic investment relationship was serially inde-

23 The rectangular lag distribution has equal weights over the total finite length
of lag.

24 The weights are obtained by dividing each of the terms in the series $1, 2, ., n/2,$
$n/2, \ldots, 2, 1$, by the sum of the series $(n^2+2n)/4$.

pendent, but none included a lagged (dependent) variable. Hence the ordinary least squares estimation problems were simply those associated with autocorrelated errors, namely: (i) the parameter estimates are unbiased, but inefficient (compared with some other estimation method); and (ii) the conventional least squares formulas for calculating the sampling variances of the regression coefficients underestimate these variances.

A further generalisation of the lag distributions considered by Fisher and de Leeuw has been applied by Lund and Holden (1968) to annual U.K. data for the period 1923–38. Their method consisted of constructing a number of alternative composite 'lagged values' of the explanatory variables based on alternative hypothetical lag distributions, and making a choice between these alternatives on the basis of their separate performances in regression equations. This was assessed by their statistical significance and the overall goodness of fit of the regression equation in which they were included. Important advantages of this method are that it does not require the coefficients of the successive lagged values of the explanatory variables to be related in any systematic way, and that it readily permits alternative lag distributions to be specified for different explanatory variables. Like Fisher's method it yields a final equation for estimation that contains neither lagged variables nor autocorrelated errors. However, as the authors admitted, it has one major disadvantage:[25]

'it is expensive with regard to computing time because many alternative combinations of the lagged values of each of the explanatory variables have to be constructed and tested in regression analysis before a final form can be accepted as satisfactory. In general the shorter the unit time period, the more alternative and conceptually feasible lag schemes (i.e. ones in which the predetermined weights attached to successive observations of each of the explanatory variables are all simple fractions, such as multiples of $\frac{1}{12}$) can be constructed and tested; thus the method is better suited for application to annual than quarterly data.'

Another possible criticism relates to the power of the minimisation of squared residuals (or maximisation of overall fit) criterion to discriminate effectively between alternative lag distributions. Unfortunately, the evidence here is not reassuring. Lund and Holden found that, for a simple capital stock adjustment model, a wide range of alternative lag distributions yielded $\bar{R}^2$ in the narrow range 0·835 to 0·864. However, this apparent weakness of the overall fit criterion should be compared with Griliches' findings on the wide variety of lag distributions which

25 Lund and Holden (1968), p. 60.

may be consistent, within sampling errors, with a single estimated equation. It seems that ultimately the choice between alternative lag distributions must be affected by their consistency or otherwise with any extraneous information about lag structure, such as has been provided by Mayer (1953, 1958, 1960), Zarnowitz (1962), and Lund (1967).

In similar vein, Lund and Holden warned of the dangers that arise in estimating a distributed lag function between, say, two variables when those variables have been simultaneously effected by some other variable, or random shock. Suppose, for example, that I and X are linked by some distributed lag scheme, such that only previous values of X affect I:

$$I_t = \sum_{i=1}^{i=n} \beta(w_i \, X_{t-i}), \text{ where } n \text{ is the maximum lag.}$$

If there is a third variable, Z, such that $I_t = f(Z_t)$ and $X_t = f(Z_t)$ but other values of Z have no effect on I or X, then I_t and X_t will be correlated. Hence, unless the method of estimating the distributed lag function incorporates the specification $w_0 = 0$ or includes the variable Z_t, some weight is likely to be attached to X_t, and the estimated shape of the lag distribution will be biased towards the shorter lags. This reasoning, expounded by Lund and Holden with reference to the effects of the British 1926 general strike on variables such as investment, profits and capacity utilisation, may explain why many econometric studies of investment have given estimates of average lags much less than those suggested by the statistical and questionnaire studies. Another reason is that simultaneous interaction tends to increase the measured correlation of those regressions which include explanatory variables of the current time period, without necessarily implying a better explanation of the causal demand relationship.

The final method of estimating a stable lag distribution to be discussed in this section is that due to Almon (1965). The fundamental idea underlying her method is to estimate the weights corresponding to a few points on the lag distribution curve, and to use polynomial interpolation to derive estimates of the remaining weights. The steps in the method may be summarised as follows:

(i)   Choose a reasonable range of values for n, the total length in unit periods of the lag distribution. The estimation method is applied for each of these values of n, and the choice between them governed by the criteria described after step (vi).

(ii) Choose a value of q, where $q+1$ is the degree of the polynomial considered to be sufficient to allow a close approximation to the true lag distribution.

(iii) Choose the location of q points, to be denoted by X_j, $j = 1 \ldots q$, in the interval between a lag of 0 and a lag of n. The choice of these points does not materially affect the resulting estimates. These q points are sufficient to locate a polynomial of degree $q+1$, since the weights corresponding to the points $(t+1)$ and $(t-n)$ are specified in advance to be zero.

(iv) Use lagrangian interpolation coefficients to convert the observations on the n variables corresponding to the n lagged values of X into observations on q variables each of which are different linear combinations of the lagged X values.

(v) Regress I_t on these q variables, obtaining estimates of the coefficients of the q variables, and then derive the weights as linear combinations of these estimates.

(vi) Vary n over the chosen range, repeating steps (i)–(v).

The choice between the alternative values of n, and their corresponding lag distributions, is made according to two criteria. The first is overall fit; however this is not very discriminating since the difference between the best and worst distributions is usually very small. In studying the lag between investment appropriations and expenditures for 18 U.S. industries for the period 1953–61, Almon found the differences in R^2 to be between 0·02 and 0·32; for all manufacturing, it was 0·04. The second criteria is to select a value of n yielding estimates of the weights which are all non-negative and very similar to those obtained for larger values of n. Although Almon applied her method to a problem in which the effect of only one explanatory variable (investment appropriations) was considered to be distributed through time, this is not a necessary restriction, and the method could allow different polynomial distributions for each variable. However, although one of the merits of her method is that it substantially reduces multicollinearity problems in the estimating equation, the incorporation of several explanatory variables would soon lead to a serious loss of degrees of freedom and increasing problems of multicollinearity. Thus, when applying the method to studying the determinants of appropriations, using a model which included three explanatory variables, Almon (1968) assumed that their lag distributions could be approximated using a parabolic form. Almon's apparently flexible method may therefore enforce more constraints on the basic functional specification than the methods which only require one extra variable in the estimating equation for each additional variable included in the basic investment relationship. Moreover, like all of the other methods described, Almon's suffers from the serious disadvantage that it unrealistically assumes the lag distribution to be stable.

4.5. Variable Lag Distributions

Methods which allow the lag distribution to vary through time have been described by Alt (1942), Popkin (1965, 1966) and Tinsley (1967). Alt assumed that the parameters in a lag distribution, such as specified in equation (4.1), are linear functions of time. Equation (4.1) can thus be rewritten as

$$I_t = (a_0 + b_0 t) \, X_t + (a_1 + b_1 t) \, X_{t-1} + (a_2 + b_2 t) \, X_{t-2} + \ldots + u_t,$$

$$(4.40)$$

and for estimation purposes as

$$I_t = a_0 \, X_t + a_1 \, X_{t-1} + a_2 \, X_{t-2} + \ldots + b_0 t \, X_t + b_1 t \, X_{t-1} + b_2 t \, X_{t-2}$$
$$+ \ldots + u_t \qquad\qquad (4.41)$$

Unfortunately because of multicollinearity problems, only very few lagged values of X can be included in such an estimating equation, and the introduction of further explanatory variables (each with parameters assumed to be functions of time) renders estimation impracticable.

Popkin generalised Alt's suggestion by specifying that the parameters (or weights in his formulation) are a function of an economic variable. In his work on the lag distribution between investment appropriations and expenditures, Popkin assumed that the weights were a function of the ratio of appropriation backlogs (appropriations still to be transformed into actual expenditures) to expenditures at the time the appropriations were made. By so doing he was able to take account of the variations in the production (or order to delivery) period that results from variations in the pressure of demand upon the capital goods industries. However, probably in order to obtain an equation practical for estimation purposes, Popkin assumed that the lag distribution under study required only two different weights. His specification was of the form:

$$I_t = \beta[w_{i,\,t} \, X_{t-i} + w_{i-1,\,t} \, X_{t-i-1}] + u_t \qquad\qquad (4.42)$$

where

$$w_{i,\,t} = \gamma_0 + \gamma_1 \left(\frac{BL}{E}\right)_{t-i} \qquad\qquad (4.43)$$

and

$$w_{i-1,\,t+1} = 1 - w_{i,\,t} \qquad\qquad (4.44)$$

and hence

$$w_{i-1,\,t} = 1 - w_{i,\,t-1} = 1 - \left[\gamma_0 + \gamma_1 \left(\frac{BL}{E}\right)_{t-i-1}\right] \qquad (4.45)$$

Substituting equations (4.43) and (4.45) into (4.42) gives

$$I_t = \beta \left\{ \gamma_0 \, \Delta X_{t-i} + \gamma_1 \Delta \left[\left(\frac{BL}{E} \right)_{t-i} X_{t-i} \right] + X_{t-i-1} \right\} + u_t \quad (4.46)$$

The term (BL/E) is the ratio of appropriation backlogs to expenditures. Equation (4.43) relates the first non-zero weight in the lag distribution w_i to the size of this ratio at time $t-i$. Equation (4.44) constrains the weight of the second lag term in time $t+1$ to be the complement of that of the first lag term in t_1. The second weight term in equation (4.42) can therefore be expressed in terms of the first weight term, as in equation (4.45). Popkin, in fact, released this constraint when examining the lag between appropriations for investment expenditure and the subsequent expenditure. In most applications of the method, although not Popkin's own, this is probably necessary since straightforward regression estimation of equation (4.46) would result in the structural parameters β, γ_0 and γ, being overidentified. Popkin's relaxation was equivalent to placing an unconstrained coefficient of γ_2 on X_{t-i-1}, and adding a constant term to equation (4.46).

A generalisation of Popkin's method, which can also incorporate Almon's interpolation technique, has been presented by Tinsley, and applied by both him and Almon (1968). Like Alt, they assumed that the weights in the lag distribution were linear functions of some third variable, but eased the multicollinearity problem by incorporating Almon's interpolation technique. Like Popkin both studied the translation of investment appropriations into expenditures, and assumed that the weights were a function of the backlog expenditures ratio. Almon compared the lag distributions for the periods when this variable attained its highest and lowest values. Although these distributions were not markedly different, that corresponding to the higher pressure of demand was clearly the longer. A comparison of the sum of the weights suggested that the share of appropriations actually spent may well have varied over time, being greatest when the pressure of demand, and hence probably expectations about the future, were at their peak.

The methods of estimating flexible lag distributions proposed by Alt, Popkin and Tinsley represent a considerable advance in terms of realism as compared with methods which implicitly assume the lag distribution to be stable. The associated regression studies of investment conducted by Almon, Popkin and Tinsley had another important feature in common; they all considered only one stage in the investment process, that between the appropriation of funds and the subsequent expenditures. The advantage of this procedure is that the lag distribution for one stage in the investment process is obviously shorter, and hence simpler to estimate, than the convolution of the distributions for each of the stages. This point will be further elaborated in ch. 5 § 3, 4.

The availability of data on investment reaching clearly defined and separate stages in the investment process opens the possibility of examining the variations in lags by means other than regression analysis. The advantages of such methods are that they avoid the serious estimation problems associated with multicollinearity, limited degrees of freedom, lagged variables, and autocorrelated errors. The next section describes a method which may be used to examine the inter-temporal variations in the mean production period of any particular type of capital good.

4.6. First-In First-Out Method

The method[26] to be described in this section does not permit the estimation of the lag distribution as do those of Popkin and Tinsley. Rather it focuses on the inter-temporal variation in the mean lag between the start and completion of the production process. It is therefore applicable only to those types of capital goods for which the start and completion of production is recorded statistically. Moreover it is best applied to only a single type of good, or at least homogeneous group of capital goods. Only for such a type or group may the inter-temporal variations in the mean lag be expected to predominate in importance over the lag distribution at any particular point in time.

The method is therefore described with reference to some hypothetical 'goods' which are assumed to be homogeneous. The exposition which follows will be based on a simple numerical example relating to the hypothetical starts and completions series shown in table 4.1. This not only provides the easiest form of exposition, but can be used to illustrate the sort of phenomena frequently observed in the real world production of capital goods. Besides data on starts and completions, application of the method also requires knowledge of the number of goods under construction at the end of at least one time period. Most conveniently this is the time period prior to the beginning of the starts and completions series. However, if all starts are ultimately completed (a necessary assumption for the application of the method) all the end-of-period construction figures can be derived from any one of them and the starts and completions series.

26 This method was developed by the author at the University of Manchester during 1964–65. Its application to data on industrial building and housebuilding was reported in Lund (1967), and the author is grateful to the editors of *The Manchester School* for permission to reproduce much of that article here. The method was also used, with the author's consent, in a study of foreign orders for machine tools which was conducted for the Board of Trade and subsequently reported in Steuer, Ball and Eaton (1966).

Two important assumptions are necessary in order to permit the estimation of production periods from such a set of data. One, relating to the working procedures of the capital goods industries, is that goods are completed in the same order as they are started: this is the well-known first-in first-out (F.I.F.O.) assumption. The second, relating to the interpretation of the available statistical information, is that the starts and completions recorded in each unit time period are evenly spread throughout that period. The realism of these assumptions and the consequences of their non-satisfaction are discussed later in this section.

TABLE 4.1

First-in first-out method. Hypothetical example: starts and completions data and work analysis

Time period	Hypothetical goods Started	Hypothetical goods Completed	Under construction (end of period)	Assumed division of completions by period in which they were started
0	..	..	15	
1	25	20	20	15 of UC_0, 5 of S_1
2	40	25	35	20 of S_1, 5 of S_2
3	30	30	35	30 of S_2
4	15	30	20	5 of S_2, 25 of S_3
5	20	25	15	5 of S_3, 15 of S_4, 5 of S_5

Employing the first assumption—that goods are completed in the same order as they are started, it is possible to divide the total of each period's completions according to the time period in which they were started. Thus referring to table 4.1, the 20 goods completed in period 1 are assumed to consist of the 15 goods under construction at the end of period 0, and the first 5 goods started in period 1. Similarly, the 25 goods completed in period 2 are assumed to consist of the remaining 20 goods started in period 1, and the first 5 goods started in period 2. The assumed divisions of completions in the subsequent periods are derived in the same way and shown in table 4.1. It is significant that this shows the completions of period 3 to consist entirely of the starts of only one period (2), but the completions of period 5 to consist of the starts of three different periods (3, 4 and 5). An identical analysis of

United Kingdom industrial building and machine tools statistics conducted by the author showed that such a situation is not atypical. It simply reflects the differences in production periods and waiting times which have been experienced.

Employment of the second basic assumption—that the recorded starts and completions of each unit period are evenly spread throughout that period—allows the estimation of production periods for goods started or completed at any point in time. Consider the first good started in the first period: this is assumed to be the 16th good completed in the first period, and—on the basis of the second assumption can be said to have been completed 77·5% of the way through period 1, which point in time is to be denoted by 1·775. (It is assumed that not only are jobs completed at a steady rate within each period, e.g. one in each $\frac{1}{20}$th of the first period, but also that the first (and thus all) good(s) are completed at the mid-point of its (their) relevant fraction of the period; e.g. that the completions of the first period occur 2·5%, 7·5% ... 97·5% of the way through the first period.)

As the last of the goods under construction at the end of the first period—which is assumed to be the last good started during period 0—would have been completed 72·5% of the way through period 1, i.e. at point in time 1·725, it is said that a good started exactly at the beginning of period 1 (or end of period 0) would have been completed $(77\cdot5 + 72\cdot5)/2\%$ of the way through period 1, i.e. at point in time 1·750. Thus it can be said that a good started at the beginning of period 1 would have had a production period of 0·750 unit periods. Using similar reasoning, the production periods of goods assumed to have been started at any point in time can be estimated.

The production periods of goods assumed to have been completed at any point in time can also be estimated. For example, a good completed at the end of the first period would have been started 20% of the way through period 1, i.e. at point in time 1·200 and would thus have had a production period of 0·800 unit periods.

The estimated points in time at which goods assumed to have been started or completed at the beginning of each period would have been completed or started, together with the corresponding production periods are shown in table 4.2.

This type of analysis can also be performed graphically as in fig. 4.4 which shows both cumulative starts and cumulative completions plotted against the same time scale. In this fig. the upper line shows cumulative starts, the lower line cumulative completions. The cumulative starts are shown as being 15 at the beginning of period 1, because the under construction figure for the end of period 0 indicates that up to that point in time cumulative starts must have exceeded cumulative completions by 15. The joining of the individual plotted points by straight lines corresponds to the assumption that the recorded starts and completions of each unit period are evenly spread throughout that period. The vertical distance between the cumulative starts and completions lines at any point in time shows the number of goods started but not yet completed, that is under construction, at that point in time. The horizontal distance between the two lines at a certain total of cumulative starts or completions shows the production period for the good that brought the total to that particular level. The figures can also be used to estimate the production periods for goods started or completed at any point in time. For example, the production period for a good

TABLE 4.2

First-in first-out method. Hypothetical example: production periods for goods completed/started at a particular time

Point in time good started	Production period	Point in time good completed/started	Production period	Point in time good completed
..	..	1·000	0·750	1·750
1·200	0·800	2·000	0·800	2·800
2·125	0·875	3·000	1·167	4·167
2·875	1·125	4·000	1·200	5·200
3·833	1·167	5·000	0·800	5·800
5·250	0·750	6·000	..	..

started at point in time 2·0 is given by the horizontal distance between the two lines at the point where the cumulative starts line passes through the ordinate at point in time 2·0. Similarly, the production period for a building completed at point in time 2·0 is given by the horizontal distance between the two lines at the point where the cumulative completions line passes through the ordinate at point in time 2·0.

A comparison of tables 4.1 and 4.2 reveals some of the interesting characteristics of this illustrative hypothetical example. Table 4.1 shows a starts series which is more volatile than the corresponding completions series. A rate of completions more even than that of starts is achieved by the capital goods industries allowing their production periods to

E

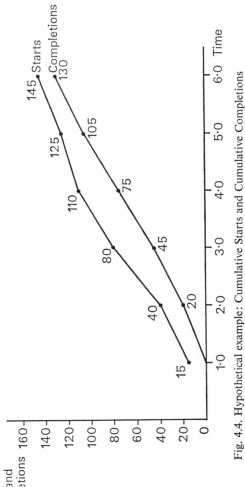

Fig. 4.4. Hypothetical example: Cumulative Starts and Cumulative Completions

lengthen (either voluntarily or involuntarily) when and just after there is a high rate of starts, and by allowing them to shorten when and just after there is a low rate of starts.

The validity of estimates of production periods derived using the method just described is dependent on the realism or unimportance of the assumptions on which the method is based. Either the assumptions must themselves be valid (at least approximately), or their non-satisfaction must have little effect on the estimates based on them.

The first assumption—that goods are completed in the same order as they are started—is not likely to be more than a very crude approximation to reality. For example, industrial buildings differ in their size, design and geographical location and machine tools in their value, complexity and uniqueness, and all of these factors may cause variations in their respective production periods. Fortunately the relaxation of this assumption does not destroy the value of the method, since however many places a particular good moves ahead of the F.I.F.O. ordering of completions, the goods following it in the starts order must (in total) move back an equal number of places in the completions order. Thus the estimates of production periods may be interpreted as the lengths of time taken to construct average goods; i.e. ones which have the same place in the completions order as in the starts order.

The realism of the second assumption—that the starts and completions recorded in each unit time period are evenly spread throughout that period—is dependent on the length of the unit time period. The shorter that period, at least up to a certain limit, the more realistic is the assumption likely to be. Of particular importance is any seasonal pattern in the starts and completions series. For example, starts and completions of industrial and commercial buildings usually show a marked seasonal variation; starts being high in spring and low in autumn and winter, and completions being high in autumn and low in spring. The construction industry clearly has a seasonal objective—to phase its work so that relatively few buildings are being built during the winter months when climatic conditions are unfavourable. This seasonal pattern implies that better estimates of the production periods of buildings may be obtained by using quarterly data than by using annual data. No marked seasonal pattern is usually evident in data on investment in machinery.

Chapter 5

ECONOMETRIC STUDIES

Econometric studies of investment can be classified into two types: those using micro-level (individual firm) data, and those using macro-level (industry or economy-wide) data. The former, which may be based either on time-series data relating to a single firm or cross-section data on a number of firms, throw some light on the decision-making processes which determine investment decisions. However, they do not necessarily provide a reliable guide to the factors which influence aggregate investment. As has already been argued some variables, such as profits and measures of competitive pressures such as changes in market share, are probably of greater relative importance at the micro level than at the macro level. That is, they determine which firms invest rather than the total industry or economy investment. Other variables, such as interest rates and tax incentives, may appear relatively unimportant at the micro level, but be of considerable significance at the macro level since they affect all firms in the same direction. In this chapter greater emphasis will therefore be given to the results of macro level than micro level regression analysis. The chapter also seeks to describe the types of data used and problems encountered in the econometric study of investment behaviour. Some suggestions for future research are made in the final section.

5.1. United Kingdom Studies

Although econometric studies of investment have been published at a prolific rate in recent years, the overwhelming majority of them have related to United States experience. Those based on United Kingdom data are few and far between, and only six have been found for discussion in this section. Of these, those by Tinbergen (1939) and Lund and Holden (1968) were estimated on the basis of aggregate data for pre World War II periods; those by Klein et al. (1961), Balopoulos (1967), and Ball and Burns (1968) form parts of complete macro-models; and that by Jack (1966) is a study at the micro-level.

Using estimated iron and steel consumption to indicate total investment, Tinbergen, after studying data for four countries including the United Kingdom for the periods 1877–1913 and 1920–1936 concluded:[1]

'there is fairly good evidence that the fluctuations in investment activity are in the main determined by the fluctuations in profits earned in industry as a whole some months earlier.'

Other variables included in the regression analysis, such as short-term interest rates, the price of iron, the rate of increase of production and prices, and profit margins, were generally found to be of far less importance. However, the coefficients on both the accelerator and short-term interest rate variables were larger for the U.K. than for the other three countries studied, which were France, Germany and the United States. In both his studies based on U.K. data (for the two separate time periods), Tinbergen included the profits variable lagged by one year; this lag not only achieved the best overall fit, but would also seem to overcome the problems associated with any two-way simultaneous causal relationship between investment and profits. However, Eisner and Strotz have cast doubts on the validity of Tinbergen's conclusion about the profits variables:[2]

'(There) is the danger that variables which appear to be related reflect in their relationship merely a common association with other unspecified factors which are involved in the true (but unrevealed) structural relation. There is always a strong danger that this is true in the case of profit, which represents a measure, albeit imperfect, of much of economic experience and, since change is not always abrupt and is in any event usually imperfectly foreseen is, in addition, positively associated with the expected values of variables such as future demand, which might also (and more reasonably) be related to investment.
    A major difficulty with lengthy time series is that many variables are likely to be moving in the same general direction (usually up) and hence will appear statistically related. Thus positive relations to investment might well have been found for not only profits within the country or industry but also profits in other countries or industries.'

As Eisner and Strotz pointed out, these criticisms apply with equal force to many other subsequent studies of investment.
    Although Tinbergen's studies suggested that interest rate variations had little effect on French, German or American investment, they did appear important in the case of U.K. investment. The coefficients on the interest rate variable (yield on $2\frac{1}{2}\%$ Consols) implied that a reduction

1 Tinbergen (1939), p. 49.
2 Eisner and Strotz (1963), pp. 140–141.

of 10% in this long-term rate would have caused a 31% increase in investment in the pre-World War I period, and a 10% increase in the inter-war period. However, the quantitative effect of interest-rate variations may not have been substantial, for as Tinbergen observed, 'the largest fall per annum in the long-term interest rate in any cycle before the war (i) was 0·18% and that in most cases was far less'.[3] Moreover Tinbergen's representative set of significance calculations suggested that, even for the earlier period, the interest-rate coefficient may not have been significant in many of the formulations estimated. On the other hand, in a study confined to investment in railway rolling-stock Tinbergen found more consistent and significant interest-rate effects. He attributed this in part to the 'considerable length of life of railway rolling-stock and in the large part of this investment which, in the end, is financed through the capital market in the proper sense of the word'.[4] On 'a priori' grounds Tinbergen also considered that the acceleration principle may be of more importance in railway investment than in total investment. He mentioned two facts which lead railway companies to replace pure profit considerations by more technical considerations so far as new investment is concerned. These are:

'(a) that railways usually are not permitted to refuse passengers or freight offered for transport and (b) that, generally, they are public enterprises or under some sort of control of public authority.'[5]

His econometric studies did in fact reveal that a much better explanation of U.K. railway rolling-stock investment was provided by a combination of the acceleration and profits principles than by profits alone. Probably because of the technical lag between orders and deliveries of locomotives and other stock, Tinbergen found that the best overall fit was obtained by lagging both explanatory variables by one and a half years. Although Tinbergen found that the acceleration principle provided a significant explanation ($r = 0·63$) of this type of investment, the regression equation implied that a 1% increase in railway traffic would result in only a 0·34% increase in rolling stock, compared with the 1% increase predicted by the crude acceleration principle.

Lund and Holden's study related to annual private sector (non-dwelling) investment during the inter-war period 1923–38. Like Tinbergen, they found that a joint profits-acceleration principle with suitable lags explained quite a large part of aggregate investment ($\overline{R}^2 =$

3 Tinbergen (1939), pp. 65–66.
4 ibid., p. 127.
5 ibid., p. 115.

0·696), but concluded that neither interest-rate nor relative factor-cost variables could meaningfully add anything to this explanation. These results are consistent with those of Radice (1939) who, using data for a similar period, found that the rate of interest did not add anything to the explanation of gross investment provided by total profits, and that net investment is a function of the rate of change of national income with a lag of about two years. Lund and Holden then incorporated expectations into the explanatory framework by adding a variable defined as 'the difference between the actual level of share prices in a year and the "normal" level associated with the current level of gross domestic product (G.D.P.).'[6] This 'normal' level was found by regressing share prices on G.D.P. for the period 1923–38, and using the regression equation to calculate the 'normal' level associated with the current level of G.D.P. Their justification for using this variable was:[7]

'in so far as they (share prices) represent expected future earnings of employed capital, their movements will reflect changes in expectations about future earnings of capital; a relatively high level of share prices indicating favourable expectations and a relatively low level indicating unfavourable expectations.'

This expectational variable proved to be significant when added to the profits-acceleration principle and also (but less so) when incorporated into the capital stock adjustment model described in ch. 2 § 9. This latter model, even without the expectational variable, provided a much better explanation of aggregate investment than did the combined profits-acceleration principle. The regression results suggested that in this model expectations may be more successfully measured by rate of change of profits than by share prices, though this finding is open to doubt since any profits variable obviously reflects availability of finance as well as expectations. Given the considerable variations in the dependent variable, the overall fit provided by the capital-stock adjustment model was relatively high; the $\overline{R}^2$ for alternative specifications reached 0·864, though as the authors pointed out, overall fit should not be the only criterion for selecting between alternative specifications.

Most of the so-called 'Oxford' model of the United Kingdom economy, developed by Klein et al., was estimated using quarterly data for 1948–56. However, the authors considered that data relating to this period was not relevant to a study of the normal determinants of investment:[8]

6 Lund and Holden (1968), p. 63.
7 ibid., p. 63.
8 Klein et al. (1961), p. 14.

'During the first years after the war (II), investment more than other economic activities was directed or forced by shortage into abnormal patterns of behaviour. Prior to 1952 it is doubtful whether anything that can be called an investment function was permitted to operate. It is generally assumed that supply and capacity limitations put a rigid ceiling on the amount of investment activity. After 1952, however, and certainly in recent years, investment has spurted ahead or been held in check according to standard economic calculations.'

The investment relationship was therefore estimated using data for only the five years, 1952–56. Moreover, because quarterly investment figures were only available for 1954 onwards, a proxy investment series had to be constructed by averaging the components of the index of industrial production relating to the metals, engineering and vehicles, and building and contracting series. Unfortunately, the resulting series included not only capital goods ultimately purchased by firms, but also those purchased by government, some goods which were to be exported, and some consumer durables. The specification of the investment relationship therefore had to incorporate all these components of final demand. The determinants of business investment were assumed to be profits, adjusted for changes in both taxes and in the prices of capital goods, and the long-term interest rate measured by a debenture yield. The interest rate variable was lagged by four quarters, and the profits variable, considering its method of construction, effectively by three quarters. The profits variable proved to be significant but the coefficient of the interest rate variable, although of correct sign, was very close to zero.

Balopoulos (1967) incorporated an equation explaining gross productive private investment into an econometric model of British fiscal policy. This dependent variable was well explained ($R^2 = 0.962$), using annual data, by the current and lagged values of gross national product net of public authorities purchases of goods and services on current account and a variable combining both the investment and initial tax allowances. In the construction of the latter variable, the existing investment and initial allowances were weighted by the present values of a £1 allowance of each type according to assumptions about the expected length of asset life and the future rate of interest. This variable, although of correct sign, proved to be statistically significant only when the lagged gross national product variable was dropped from the equation.

A distributed lag accelerator formulation was also adopted by Ball and Burns (1968) for use in their short-run forecasting model. The fitted form, which well explained quarterly data for 1955–66 ($\overline{R}^2 = 0.967$) included not only the three most recent changes in gross domestic product and two lagged values of the dependent variable but also the ratio of current gross domestic product to its trend value. This latter variable, which proved to be significant, implicitly takes account of some of the criticisms of the acceleration principle, particularly those relating to excess capacity, and hence modified it into some form of capital stock adjustment model.

Jack's study related to a total of 45 firms for the years 1963 and 1964. The information was obtained from a sample of Exchange Telegraph cards which contain a summary of the financial statements of public companies. Investment was assumed to result from the interaction of demand and supply forces, the demand for capital equipment and the supply of funds for investment purposes. Demand for net investment was assumed to be a linear function of the excess of current and recent sales over their previous peak, whilst a liquidity constraint was considered to operate only when the earnings to dividend ratio fell below a specified value. In order to avoid the problems associated with heteroscedasticity[9] each of the variables were measured in ratio form; thus the rate of change of capital stock was expressed as a function of the rate of change of sales. The need for replacement investment was indicated by the ratio of a firm's depreciation expense to its gross fixed assets. The role of profits in Jack's formulation can, at best, be described as ambiguous. After dismissing profits 'because they did not perform well in the studies conducted by Meyer and Kuh (which these authors would probably dispute) and Eisner',[10] he took advantage of the usually observed correlation between profits and sales figures to replace the unavailable sales variables in his formulation by profits variables. Jack did recognise that this procedure was open to criticism, but claimed that the following argument effectively answered such criticisms:[11]

'This study has sought to elucidate the causes of investment in a sample of

9 Heteroscedasticity is the name given to the occurrence of non-constant error variance in a regression model. It therefore invalidates one of the basic assumptions of regression analysis, which is that the error terms all come from the same distribution. Its consequence is that although the least-squares estimators are still unbiased, they do not have minimum variance. One particularly common form of heteroscedasticity is that the absolute values of the error terms are correlated with the dependent variable. For example, in a micro-level consumption function, only persons with large incomes and hence substantial consumption, may be expected to have the freedom of choice to allow their consumption to diverge markedly from that predicted by their income. However, although the errors in predicting absolute consumption may be heteroscedastic in this way, the errors in predicting consumption ratios, i.e. personal consumption expressed as a proportion of personal income, may be homoscedastic. The procedure used by Jack is equivalent to this.

10 Jack (1966), p. 141.

11 ibid., p. 157.

firms which has experienced growth of sales; in other words, it was concerned with circumstances in which Eisner and Meyer and Kuh found the acceleration hypothesis superior to profits and liquidity flow formulations. The aim of the project was not to mediate between profits and acceleration theories, but to explore the dynamics and limitations of a particular acceleration hypothesis in an investment situation which previous work had shown to be explicable in terms of acceleration reasoning. To put the point in a different way, a study of previous work in the field led to the conviction that acceleration pressure was the sole cause of "induced" investment, and it was only logical to test the resulting specification where, by hypothesis, it was applicable.'

Jack's statement that the acceleration principle has been proved superior to various profits formulations in times of business expansion is at least questionable. Moreover it appears to be inconsistent with his own results. The liquidity variable, like the profits and depreciation expense variables, proved to have significant coefficients. Thus, any supporter of the profits or liquidity theories could reasonably interpret Jack's econometric results as being significant evidence in favour of his point of view.

The variables which these regression studies of United Kingdom investment suggest to be of most importance are profits and accelerator measures. Only Tinbergen's study provided even tentative support for the theories including the rate of interest as a key variable, and Balopoulos' specific study of tax incentives yielded inconclusive results. Thus as the interview and questionnaire studies suggested, British businessmen do not seem to be sensitive to marginalist considerations.

5.2. United States Studies

'The basic position of the accelerationists is that capital goods must be loved to be worth purchasing. The basic position of the profiteers is that capital goods cannot be bought for love, alas, but only for money.'[12]

The controversy between the proponents of the acceleration principle (in its modified forms) and those supporting various profits or liquidity theories has often appeared as a central feature in U.S. econometric studies of investment behaviour. Such studies have been published at a prolific rate, several authors having recently fitted alternative regression formulations to the same basic set of data. Fortunately, a comprehensive survey of the literature through to mid-1961 has been provided by Eisner and Strotz (1963), and other summaries and commentaries by

12 Anderson (1967), p. 413.

Meyer and Kuh (1957) and Kuh (1963a). This section therefore does not seek to duplicate their work of critical evaluation, but merely to provide a guide to the main conclusions reported in this extensive literature.

Amongst the first studies of aggregate investment in the United States were those of Tinbergen (1939), Liu and Chang (1950), Klein (1950), and Klein and Goldberger (1955). Tinbergen's analysis of aggregate U.S. data was conducted alongside his work on the U.K. data, and he reached broadly similar conclusions for both countries. However, for the U.S., both the accelerator and short-term interest rate coefficients were insignificant, though a share yield variable did prove significant. Liu and Chang found that 'fluctuations in pre-war (II) investment can be more or less satisfactorily explained by movements in national product and corporation profits after taxes'.[13] Klein, in his construction of an annual model for the U.S. economy, 1929–41, fitted an investment function in which both current and lagged profits and the existing capital stock appeared as explanatory variables with significant coefficients. A similar relationship was incorporated in the Klein–Goldberger model fitted for the years 1929–41 and 1946–50. However, their formulation included a liquidity stock as well as a liquidity-flow variable; but although of correct sign, its coefficient was not statistically significant. Although all these findings appear consistent with 'profits' theories, Eisner and Strotz have argued that those associated with Klein can also be interpreted in terms of a capacity formulation of the acceleration principle.

For reasons of data availability, most of the earliest studies conducted at the industry level were concerned with the privately-owned but publicly-regulated railroad and electric power industries. For reasons already stated, Tinbergen considered that the acceleration principle is most likely to be realistic in such industries. Moreover, Kisselgoff and Modigliani later argued that profits play a less important role in monopolistic and regulated industries:[14]

'It has frequently been suggested that the productivity of capital can be approximated by the level of realised profits. . . . However, in monopolistic industries a high level of realised profits (i.e. a high average productivity of capital need not be a reliable measure of the marginal productivity of investments, which presumably controls capital outlays; indeed the high level of profits may simply reflect the successful exploitation of the monopoly power which may be "spoiled" by an expansion. These considerations apply with particular force to regulated industries . . . where firms are usually without

13 Liu and Chang (1950), p. 566.
14 Kisselgoff and Modigliani (1957), p. 364.

direct competition in their service areas and are subject to various controls which greatly affect, directly and indirectly, the level of their profits and the conditions under which the profits are obtained.'

Despite these considerations, Tinbergen found that the acceleration principle could add nothing to the explanation of U.S. investment in railway rolling-stock which was provided by two differently lagged profits variables. However, using very similar data, Manne showed that a modified version of the acceleration principle, which took account of the effects of excess capacity and uncertainty, could provide much better results than the crude version tested by Tinbergen. Further evidence supporting the 'profits' principle was then supplied by Klein (1951), who obtained a very good explanation of total annual railroad investment by using profits (measured by net operating income before depreciation), bond yield, capital stock and price index of railway capital goods of the previous year as explanatory variables. Although the coefficients of all these variables were significant and of 'correct' sign in the preferred formulation, that of the bond yield variable was found to be particularly sensitive to alternative specifications, becoming positive when the capital stock variable was omitted, and insignificant when further profits variables were added. Moreover, when this equation was re-estimated by Kmenta and Williamson (1966) using more recently available data, the coefficient became positive. Klein obtained similar results from an analysis of cross-section data for various years; the profits variable was always significant, but the interest rate variable used to reflect differences in company credit-worthiness was insignificant. He claimed that the time-series and cross-section studies together showed that 'there can be no doubt about the influence of profit on investment'.[15] However, the coefficients of additional variables reflecting the availability of finance such as net non-operating income and unappropriated surplus proved to be insignificant and often of incorrect sign. Moreover Eisner and Strotz have not only pointed out that operating profits as defined by Klein are closely related to output, but also that with this interpretation (and a little stretch of one's imagination), his formulation can be rewritten as a capital stock adjustment model. Whilst this may be too sceptical, Klein's results are certainly consistent with the hypothesis that previous profits are important merely as an indication of expected future profits, and not as a source of funds. Klein adopted the same basic formulation when studying annual investment in the electric power industry for the period 1921–41. The results of this study are not easy to interpret, for although profits proved to be

15 Klein (1951), p. 276.

highly significant, Klein replaced them in an alternative formulation by the average yield on utility shares, which variable not only proved highly significant, but also increased the overall fit. The cavalier approach to lag specification, common in studies of investment prior to about 1960, is well illustrated by this study. Although the average yield on new bonds (unlagged) proved significant in the first formulation, Klein lagged it in the second 'for the sake of variety'.[16]

Another study based on the electric power industry, and using time-series data for the period 1926–41, was conducted by Kisselgoff and Modigliani (1957). Contrary to Klein, they found that 'profits and interest rates alone completely fail to account for investment behaviour of electrical utilities',[17] whereas profits combined with a capacity formulation of the acceleration principle provided a very good explanation. This study took specific and careful account of the institutional factors affecting the industry. The long planning and gestation period determined the lag structure; and this factor together with the individuality of fixed assets, the rapid growth of demand, and the impossibility of storing the product, necessitated an allowance for a considerable normal margin of spare capacity. A distinction was also made between investment in plant and in equipment; for the latter the lags were found to be shorter and the influence of profits greater. In this study, profits were considered to play two roles, being:[18]

'an enabling factor, to the extent that it can be a source of funds from current operations for investment purposes, and of a controlling factor, to the extent that the net income component might reflect short-run business-expectations and lead to the cancellation, postponement, or acceleration of investment plans.'

The former role would suggest that profits should be lagged, the latter that they should be current. Since current profits were generally more significant than lagged profits, it appears that the latter role was the more important.

This commendable practice of incorporating institutional and technical characteristics into an investment relationship was continued by Kmenta and Williamson who distinguished between three separate periods in the life-cycle of the U.S. railroad industry. On the basis of 'a priori' reasoning, different formulations were specified for the stages of adolescence 1872–95, maturity 1895–1914, and senility 1922–41.

16 ibid., p. 280.
17 Kisselgoff and Modigliani (1957), p. 361.
18 ibid., p. 368.

Capital stock adjustment models, with and without an operating income variable, were specified for the first and second stages respectively; whilst in the latter period, profits and the size of the capital stock were used as explanatory variables. Each of these was found to be satisfactory in its own time period, whereas the application of Klein's formulation to the three periods only gave satisfactory results for the period of senility for which it was originally estimated.

A similar distinction had been made earlier by Koyck (1954) in his study of the railroad industry. Distinguishing between an 'expansionary period' (1894–1915) and a 'contraction period' (1920–29), his results confirmed the 'a priori' expectation that the acceleration principle would be more applicable in the expansionary stages of industrial development when there is less excess capacity and fewer declines in output than normal. Indeed, after applying a geometrically-declining distributed lag version of the acceleration principle to several industries, he concluded that 'the most favourable case for the acceleration principle (though not very favourable after all) is that of railway freight traffic before the first world war'[19]—the illustration given by J. M. Clark.

Intensive analysis of micro data began with the pioneering work of Meyer and Kuh (1955, 1957). They analysed data on the capital expenditures of over 700 firms in 15 industrial groupings within manufacturing industry for the period 1946–50. Their basic technique was that of simple zero-order correlation. They correlated capital expenditure in each industry and in each year separately with a large number of different possible explanatory variables, thus obtaining a total of 75 correlation coefficients for each variable. Most of their conclusions were drawn from an analysis of the distributions of these coefficients. This technique is unsatisfactory in that neither the strength nor direction of the combined effects of a number of variables can be determined from their zero-order correlation coefficients. Moreover, Meyer and Kuh almost completely ignored the time lag problem. Their results were also somewhat ambiguous. They reported:[20]

'in 1946 and 1947, when demand was expanding rapidly and liquidity was plentiful, a capacity formulation of the accelerator had by far the closest relationship with investment . . . (but) . . . in 1948 and 1949, when economic conditions stabilised, or declined in several lines of activity, two liquidity flow variables, profits and depreciation expense, provided the best explanation of investment outlay.'

19 Koyck (1954), p. 109.
20 Meyer and Kuh (1955), p. 229.

From this and an examination of the individual industry results for 1948 they concluded:[21]

'that plentiful liquidity of all the basic assumptions, seemed most essential to the accelerator's effectiveness and that, once liquidity became somewhat pinched, the availability of funds became a crucially important determinant of investment outlay in and of itself.'

On the other hand, a liquidity stock variable appeared to be uncorrelated to investment in any year, and on the basis of correlations with 5-year averaged data, Meyer and Kuh reported:[22]

'a clear tendency for liquidity and financial considerations to dominate the investment decision in the short run, while, in the long run, outlays on plant and equipment seem geared to maintenance of some relation between output and the capital stock.'

In regression studies for three industries using time-series data, they found that the unlagged yield on industrial bonds generally had a positive coefficient, but that lagged indices of industrial stock prices tended to be both positive and significant. In explaining the latter result they did not suggest that firms respond immediately to changes in the market value of their shares by making new issues but simply that the stock market probably reflects business expectations.

Meyer and Kuh's study and findings has been widely criticised, notably by Morrissett (1957) and Eisner and Strotz (1963). Both were particularly critical of Meyer and Kuh's conclusion that the relative importance of acceleration and liquidity variables fluctuates cyclically, liquidity being most important in the downturn. This criticism appears to have been substantiated by the subsequent study of Meyer and Glauber (1964) which, following a similar approach to that of the Meyer-Kuh study, found no consistent relationship between their alternative explanatory powers and cyclical state. Moreover, another study by Meyer and Kuh (1963) suggested that liquidity only becomes a problem in the later stages of the upswing, and that external funds are sought mainly at this stage of the cycle. In a further intensive study of data relating to 60 firms over a 20-year period, Kuh (1963b) incorporated both time-series and cross-section analysis, and emphasising the time-series results concluded:[23]

'no matter how the contrasts are drawn from time series, the acceleration sales model is superior to the internal fund flow, profits model.'

21 ibid., p. 230.
22 Meyer and Kuh (1957), pp. 190–191.
23 Kuh (1963b), p. 213.

This study did use multiple regression techniques, a wide variety of alternative formulations being estimated, but the lag specifications still appeared weak. However, Kuh reported that 'the statistical significance of profits is much greater when lagged'[24] and hence 'it is appropriate to view internal liquidity flows as a critical part of the budgeting process which later is modified, primarily in light of variations in the level of output and capacity utilisation'.[25] Kuh also considered the statistical problems involved in extrapolating results based on cross-section data into a time-series context, and concluded:[26]

'In general, dynamic coefficients cannot be estimated from cross-sections with any degree of confidence unless there is supporting time-series information to provide assurance that the biases (due to specification errors, different rates of adjustment, etc.) . . . do not distort the estimated coefficients and variances in the particular cross-section. Only when supporting time series are at hand can cross-sections be used safely in a time-series context.'

A time-series study of eight large corporations, using data for the period 1935–1954, was conducted by Grunfeld (1960). He found that a firm's investment could be explained by its market value, and its stock of plant and equipment, and that 'realised profits fail to incorporate the main expectation factors or liquidity considerations that determine the investment decisions of the firm'.[27] Grunfeld's model was compared by Griliches and Wallace (1965) with a model including four lagged values of sales, the firm's capital stock, and an interest rate variable. Although they found that it provided the more satisfactory explanation of the original data, its predictive performance for 1955–60 data was inferior to that of the sales model. Griliches and Wallace also developed Grunfeld's model at the aggregate level; they measured the market value of firms by a stock market price index and included an industrial bond yield, both of which proved significant.

Further evidence supporting the often-rejected interest rate theories of investment was provided in an interesting article by Gehrels and Wiggins (1957). Using half-yearly data on manufacturing industry investment, 1948–55, they not only estimated alternative investment demand equations, but also explicitly and simultaneously considered the supply of investment goods relationship. Single-equation studies of investment showed that a good overall fit could be provided by profits, the industrial bond yield, and the relative price index of capital goods,

24 ibid., p. 241.
25 ibid., p. 242.
26 ibid., p. 188.
27 Grunfeld (1958), p. 3.

each lagged by one year. However, although the coefficients of the profits and interest rate variables were of correct sign, they were insignificant, and the price index had an (incorrect) positive sign. But as Gehrels and Wiggins argued, the price of capital goods has a two-way relationship with investment, and this is likely to be such that current investment, reflecting orders placed a year before, had an effect on the price of capital goods lagged by one year. Because of the close interdependence of current investment and lagged new orders, the normal econometric assumption of no simultaneity between current dependent and lagged independent variables breaks down in this case. Recognition of this factor prompted Gehrels and Wiggins to specify a simultaneous model containing an investment supply relationship with lagged prices (of capital goods) and hourly wage rates as explanatory variables. The coefficients of the investment demand equation, derived from the reduced-form estimates were of correct sign, though generally insignificant. However, a similar formulation for the immediate pre-war (II) period yielded an investment demand equation in which the profits variable had a negative sign, and the economic explanations of this provided by Gehrels and Wiggins appear unconvincing.

Meanwhile, statistical examination of the acceleration and capacity theories was being conducted concurrently by Chenery (1952), Eisner (1960), de Leeuw (1962) and Hickman (1965). Chenery compared the explanatory power of the capital stock adjustment model described in ch. 2 § 9 with that of the acceleration principle, using inter-war data on six industries (electricity, steel, cement, zinc, petroleum and paper). He reported:[28]

'on an overall basis, the capacity principle showed reasonable success ($r > 0.65$) for all the industries tested, while the accelerator was quite inadequate in half of them. However, in two cases, petroleum and paper, the accelerator was slightly better than the capacity explanation.'

Chenery offered differences in industrial structure as an explanation:[29]

'If entry is not hampered by large capital requirements, an expanding demand may attract new firms even if there is already over-capacity in the industry, particularly if technological change gives them some advantage over older plants. This possibility favours the acceleration explanation over the capacity formula. On the other hand, if expansion of capital is made almost entirely by firms already in the industry, they may be expected to take account of the existing degree of excess capacity. The capacity principle may be thought

28 Chenery (1952), p. 21.
29 ibid., p. 20.

of as applying particularly to oligopolies and industries with high capital intensities, while the accelerator more nearly fits competitive markets and production functions permitting lower capital coefficients. Steel, cement, electricity, zinc fall in the former categories, while paper and petroleum refining are more nearly in the latter.'

For each industry and each formulation, Chenery selected the appropriate lag structure as being that which yielded the best overall fit, and these were generally very short. Eisner and Strotz have commented adversely:[30]

'This, along with . . . higher coefficients in growing industries, suggests the possibility that increases in capacity made possible and hence induced increases in output, rather than the reverse.'

Eisner utilised the accounts of some 200 large corporations for the years 1953–55 to estimate the distributed lag effects of sales changes on investment. Although simple correlations between investment and profits were positive, he argued that:[31]

'These positive relations were entirely accounted for and were not manifested as significantly positive regression coefficients when current and three lagged sales changes were included in the regression. This is clearly consistent with the hypothesis that firms with high profits invest more, not because of the high profits per se, but because firms with high profits tend to be those which have been experiencing sales increases over a number of years and have reason therefore to expand capacity.'

However, after comparing regression results for the third of the firms that had experienced the greatest long run sales expansion with those for the others, Eisner admitted:[32]

'Findings are consistent with the hypothesis that the accelerator is non-linear in character. Its effect is apparently concentrated among firms whose sales have been rising and who have had relatively rapid long-term rates of growth.'

In more recent work (1963, 1967) Eisner has developed and statistically explored a permanent income version of the accelerator principle, and argued that:[33]

30 Eisner and Strotz (1963), p. 147.
31 ibid., p. 176.
32 Eisner (1960), p. 28.
33 Eisner (1963), p. 238.

'investment is a stable function of "permanent" changes in output and that enigmatic results of many past investigators have stemmed from attempts to estimate the unstable proxy relation including large elements of "transitory" changes in income.'

Unfortunately Eisner's method of distinguishing between permanent and transitory changes appears unsatisfactory:[34]

'we assume that businessmen recognise that departures of their own experience from concurrent experiences of the industry are likely to be in large part random and transitory in character, while interindustry and intertemporal differences will reflect in much greater proportion long-run or permanent factors.'

However, his regression results confirm his hypothesis that, when studying individual firm data, the acceleration coefficient on industry sales-changes, would be greater than that on the alternative, the firm's sales changes.

De Leeuw (1962), returning to the Keynesian concept of a marginal efficiency of capital schedule, identified changes in output, in the degree of excess capacity, and in the rate at which capital is wearing out, as factors causing shifts in the schedule. The availability and cost of funds were measured by internal funds and the industrial bond yield respectively. De Leeuw combined the specification of capital requirements described in ch. 2 § 9 with the method of estimating a distributed lag function presented in ch. 4 § 4. In a study of quarterly data for manufacturing industry 1947–50, he found that the coefficients of his capital requirements variable, internal funds and bond yields were all of correct sign and statistically significant, and that the best overall fit was provided by an inverted-V distribution extending over twelve quarters. In an extension of de Leeuw's model to further data, Eckstein (1965) dropped the assumption that output is expected to grow at a constant annual rate and added specific variables to reflect business expectations. Two alternatives, the change in unfilled orders and a comprehensive index of leading business cycle indicators, improved the overall fit and had satisfactory and significant coefficients. However, the introduction of the latter rendered the internal funds coefficient insignificant and of wrong sign, and this led Eckstein to suggest that 'the internal flow of funds . . . may partly play the role of a proxy for the general business outlook.'[35]

34 ibid., p. 240.
35 Eckstein (1965), p. 422.

Hickman, in a study of annual 1949–60 data for separate industries, used an adjustment model in which the desired capital stock was determined by current and previous values of output and a real price of capital variable (compounded from indices of product and capital goods prices and data on interest and depreciation rates). Although alternative variants of the price variable were tested, Hickman reported that 'in most sectors the price variables were of the wrong sign, were statistically insignificant, or both'.[36] Dropping this variable reduced Hickman's formulation to a complex accelerator model which provided only modest explanations for some industries and which made greater errors in forecasting 1961 and 1962 data than a simple naive model.[37]

Another model which has had poor forecasting success is that developed by Anderson (1964). Like de Leeuw, Anderson returned to the Keynesian version of the neoclassical theory, characterising his model as:[38]

'a restatement of the neoclassical position that investment is determined by the intersection of the marginal efficiency schedule with the marginal cost of funds schedule. The marginal efficiency schedule . . . shifts about primarily in response to changes in the rate of utilisation of existing capacity. The marginal cost of funds schedule shifts about in response to changes in the degree of financial risk as well as to changes in the market cost of funds.'

He laid particular stress on financial variables including, amongst a long list of investment determining factors, variables accounting for 'the relationship between existing debt and the maximum allowable, the relationship between actual and desired liquidity, and the borrowing and lending rates of interest'.[39] These in turn were measured by short-term bank debt and long-term debt capacity (defined as the difference between 18 % of total assets and outstanding long-term debt); by stocks of cash and government securities, and level of sales, accrued tax liability and outstanding short-term debt; and by the yields on industrial bonds and treasury bills. After estimating that part of the investment lag structure corresponding to the actual production period, Anderson used a weighted average of the values of these explanatory variables lagged between four and seven quarters to explain investment. His time series study for the period 1948–59 related to manufacturing industries,

36 Hickman (1965), p. 53.
37 A naive model is one which forecasts future values of a variable by some simple extrapolation of its past values. Hickman used the actual value in the previous year as a naive forecast.
38 Anderson (1964), p. 37.
39 ibid., p. 70.

both as a whole and separately, and was unusual in that the data were not price-deflated. Of his long list of financial variables, preliminary analysis at the aggregate level showed that the most important were stocks of government securities, accrued tax liability, long-term debt capacity and the yield on treasury bills. Other explanatory variables were a measure of capacity utilisation (the difference between sales and their previous maximum level), gross retained profits and a time trend.

The model formulated by Jorgenson and summarised in ch. 2 § 3 has been used by Jorgenson and Stephenson (1967a, b) to explain investment within separate manufacturing industries during the period 1947–60, and to examine the shape of the lag distribution. Hall and Jorgenson (1967) have also used it specifically to assess the effectiveness of tax policies designed to stimulate investment. However, despite its achievements of high explanatory power and 'a priori' reasonable estimates of lag distributions, doubts must remain concerning this model. Since few businessmen can be assumed to possess Jorgenson's intellectual armoury, the model must be interpreted as explaining the results of business behaviour rather than the way businessmen actually determine their investment decisions. Moreover, an important statistical criticism arises since all the variables supposed to affect net investment are incorporated into a single composite variable, and Jorgenson attributes the significance and explanatory strength of this composite to each of its separate components. This is a very dubious procedure especially since the composite variable includes the level of output, for if this alone were significant, the model would be reduced merely to a complex version of the acceleration principle. Finally, an examination of the diagrams presented in Jorgenson and Stephenson (1967b), showing the contribution of the different variables (change in desired capital stock, lagged net investment, capital stock) to the explanation of gross investment, is very revealing. For all industries the two lagged dependent variables contribute most of the explanatory power, whilst the effects of changes in the desired capital stock are frequently swamped by the residual errors. On the other hand, a comparison of five alternative models made by Jorgenson and Siebert (1968), using time-series data on 15 large corporations and the same distributed lag scheme for each model, found two alternative formulations of the neoclassical theory to be superior to three models equating the desired capital stock with output (accelerator), the flow of internal funds (liquidity) and the market value of the firm (profits expectations).

Further analysis of quarterly-data for separate manufacturing industries has been conducted by Evans (1967), and Resek (1966). Evans, after considering both the formation of original plans and their subsequent revision at the individual firm level, postulated a bi-modal lagged response at the aggregate level. He found that it gave 'significant coefficients in almost all cases, although other functions might have given equally good results'.[40] After comparing results for 13 manufacturing and 6 non-manufacturing industries, he concluded that both cash flow and interest rates were important in the manufacturing sector, whilst the interest rate was clearly the only important financial variable in non-manufacturing. Resek experimented with alternative specifications of the acceleration principle and alternative measures of the cost of funds. He found that investment (relative to existing capital stock) was most satisfactorily explained by the Almon-weighted lagged values of the change in output (relative to capital stock), a general rate of interest, the debt minus retained funds to assets ratio, and the industry's stock market price index. As in a similar study conducted by Lintner (1967), no significant effects could be found for any of several alternative measures reflecting the relative costs of capital goods.

It is not easy to reconcile all these empirical studies, at least in the sense of emphatically proving or disproving the validity of individual theories of investment behaviour. Indeed the often conflicting nature of their results suggest that investment is a complex process which cannot be expressed by such simple theories as those propagated by extreme accelerationists or profiteers. On the other hand, the neo-classical theory of Jorgenson with its implicit assumption of a world of unemotional rational businessmen may well be 'too clever by half'. Businessmen, like other human beings, have prejudices and changes in mood and a realistic theory of investment behaviour should incorporate these characteristics.

Substantial statistical problems have been encountered in attempting to discriminate between alternative theories of aggregate investment. Alternative theories may fit the available data equally well. Indeed, regression analysis may be unable to discriminate between alternative theories since they may reduce to the same basic equation for estimation purposes. Multicollinearity, especially between sales, output and profits, so hinders attempts to discriminate on the basis of aggregate data that recourse is sometimes taken to micro-data, despite the problems involved in translating even clear-cut micro-level results into meaningful conclusions about aggregate behaviour. Multicollinearity also increases the danger that an apparently significant variable is standing as a proxy for the true but unspecified determining variables. This danger is greatest if the lag structure is not carefully specified on 'a priori' grounds,

40 Evans (1967), p. 163.

with certain restrictions about its length and shape being imposed. The next section discusses an approach whereby the problems associated with the estimation of complex, lengthy and variable lag distributions may be considerably reduced.

5.3. Two-Stage Studies of Investment

The problems associated with estimating distributed lag functions using econometric methods were discussed in ch. 4 § 1–5. Although a wide variety of estimation methods have been proposed, none can be considered wholly satisfactory for studying investment behaviour. The fundamental difficulty arises from the length of the lag distribution, since it is impracticable for all the relevant lagged values to be included in a single equation. Those methods of estimating stable lag distributions which avoid this problem by imposing a certain form of lag distribution are subject to other problems of estimation or interpretation. Whilst the methods which allow variation in the lag distribution are more realistic, they are especially prone to problems of multicollinearity and limited degrees of freedom since they introduce further variables into the equation to be estimated. Partly because of these intransigent problems, some econometricians have split the investment process into two stages, and studied each of (or one of) the stages separately. The first stage is that between the factors which influence the decision to invest and the first revealed intentions of investment (ex ante data); the second stage is that which leads on to actual investment expenditure (ex post data).

Econometricians working with aggregate United States data have usually identified the end of the first stage with one of three sets of data. These are: (i) the government's survey of business investment anticipations conducted jointly by the Office of Business Economics of the Department of Commerce and the Securities and Exchange Commission; (ii) the surveys of business plans for investment in new plant and equipment collected by the McGraw-Hill Publishing Co.; (iii) the series, collected and reported by the National Industrial Conference Board, on the capital appropriations of large manufacturing corporations that have formulated capital budgeting procedures.

The anticipations series are different in concept from the appropriations series. The appropriations series indicate aggregate investment which is currently passing through a certain stage in the investment process, and which is likely to be translated into actual expenditures in some future but as yet unspecified period. The investment anticipations and intentions series constitute a forecast of expenditures in some specific future period on investment projects which may currently be at different stages in the investment process. However the two types of series are similar in that both may be of considerable value in studying the determinants of investment and in forecasting future investment. Appropriations data are likely to be of the greater value when studying the determinants of investment since they provide the earliest indication of investment decisions, and thus minimise the length and complexity of the lag distribution at the first stage. They allow the equation describing the first stage to contain only few current or lagged values of each of the several explanatory variables, and that for the second stage to include only lagged values of appropriations. By separating the complex part of the lag distribution from the several explanatory variables, the use of appropriations data considerably reduces the estimation problems associated with multicollinearity and limited degrees of freedom. Anticipations data is likely to be of the greater value when the aim is simply to forecast future investment since they provide a straightforward forecast for specific future periods.

If the aim is to forecast, it may be possible to concentrate on this second stage in the investment process, and ignore the determination of investment appropriations or intentions altogether. Such a forecasting procedure may be described as 'forecasting without understanding', but since the test of a forecasting model is simply whether or not it works (i.e. its ability to make good forecasts), this comment need not imply criticism. Of course, a complete forecasting model may include a relationship describing the first stage in the investment process, and hence yielding forecasts of investment appropriations or intentions, but this is not necessary. Given the controversy concerning the determinants of investment, the efficiency of a forecasting model may be greater if the first stage is ignored. The only major disadvantage of confining attention to the second stage is that the number of future periods for which forecasts can be made may be reduced.

If the forecasting model is limited to the second stage, the appropriations or intentions series may be utilised in various alternative ways. One alternative is simply to postulate that investment expenditure in some future period is exactly equal to current appropriations or intentions; for the intentions series this would imply accepting them simply at their face-value. Alternatively, and especially for the appropriations series, it may be assumed that the expenditures generated by the appropriations or intentions will be distributed through time, and the form of the distributed lag function may be estimated using one of the methods described in ch. 4. This procedure may, however, prove unsatisfactory for a number of reasons. Firstly, the appropriations or intentions

series may be a biased estimate of future expenditures. Actual investment may exceed or fall short of appropriations because some investment may be made without appropriation or because of cancellations.
Similarly, the investment intentions series may prove to be biased
because firms persistently under-or-over-estimate their future investment. Secondly, firms may decide to revise their investment plans in the
light of subsequent experience. For example, a fall in demand, even
after the appropriations stage, may cause a firm to postpone or even
cancel a proposed investment. Thirdly, because of variations in their
own pressure of demand, the capital goods industries may be forced,
or may choose, to translate appropriations or intentions into actual
expenditures at a slower or quicker rate than is normal.

All of these factors can be built into the forecasting model by specifying what is usually called a realisation function. The concept of the
realisation function was developed by Modigliani and Cohen (1958,
1961) to show that:[41]

'the discrepancies between actual and planned behaviour should largely
be accounted for by the discrepancy between the behaviour of the environment as anticipated at the time the plan was made and the actual behaviour
of the environment over the period to which the plan refers.'

For example, instead of simply equating investment expenditures with
a weighted average of previous appropriations, this could include as
extra explanatory variables both the factors affecting the investing firms
since the time appropriations were made, and factors determining the
production period for capital goods. Alternatively and especially when
the ex ante data on investment is an intentions series, these variables
may be used to explain, and hence subsequently predict, any differences
between investment intentions and actual expenditures.

The aggregate predictive performance of the U.S. anticipations series
has been assessed by various authors, including Modigliani and Weingartner (1958), who also estimated a realisation function. On the basis
of data for 1947–55, they found that the Commerce-SEC data provided
more accurate forecasts than two alternative naive models,[42] and that
their apparent tendency to underestimate actual investment 'reflects
primarily the failure to anticipate the rising price trend of the post-war
period, rather than any systematic tendency to underestimate the volume
of investments'.[43] Moreover, using a realisation function, they were

41 Modigliani and Weingartner, (1958), p. 38.
42 The two alternative naive models considered by Modigliani and Weingartner
were that investment in year t can be forecast as equal to that of year $t-1$, and occur-
ring at the same rate as that of the fourth quarter of year $t-1$.
43 Modigliani and Weingartner, (1958), p. 33.

able to explain 60% of the average discrepancy between actual investment and price-adjusted investment anticipations by errors in sales
expectations (actual sales minus expected sales). This result is partly
substantiated by the findings of Friend and Bronfenbrenner (1955) and
Eisner (1958) who analysed cross-section data, and with a table constructed by Foss and Natrella (1960) which compared errors in forecasting investment and sales for 14 manufacturing industries, 1952–56.
Eisner, who studied a sample of the McGraw-Hill data for 1948–50,
also found that 'data . . . on sales changes concurrent with revelation
of plans permitted significant improvement in investment predictions
for the medium and small (firms)',[44] but that 'profits . . . were apparently fully reflected in capital expenditure anticipations or plans.'[45]

The Brookings quarterly econometric model of the U.S. both used
anticipatory data for short-run forecasting (Eisner) and sought to
explain these anticipations so that more distant extrapolations could
be made (Jorgenson). Jorgenson, in fact, explained both actual investment and investment anticipations using his neoclassical model, and
also estimated simple lag relationships between investment and anticipations. Eisner again considered not only a realisation function in the
Modigliani-Cohen sense, but also the failure of anticipatory data to fully
reflect current experience at the time they are reported. He concluded:[46]

'Lagged sales changes were positively associated with the error in anticipations in all industries . . . A . . . quarterly sales realisation variable . . . while
also related positively to investment realisations, proved generally less useful
than changes in actual sales . . . Profits changes generally added little to the
explained variance not already accounted for by other variables and were in
some instances negatively related to the deviations between actual and anticipated expenditures'.

Both the determinants of investment appropriations and their transmission into actual expenditures have been studied by Sachs and Hart
(1967) and Almon (1965, 1968). Sachs and Hart found that expenditures
could be satisfactorily explained by appropriations through quarters
$(t-6)$ to $(t-2)$; that an eclectic model including cash-flow, bond-yield
and the ratio of orders to capacity provided a better explanation of
appropriations than either 'pure-finance' or 'accelerator' models; and
that the combination of recent cash flow, and to a lesser extent orders,
improved the explanation of expenditures provided by appropriations
alone. Almon (1965) first estimated the distributed lag pattern between
appropriations and expenditures using the method described in ch. 4

44 Eisner (1958), p. 187.
45 ibid., p. 188.
46 Eisner (1965), p. 127.

§ 4, and then (1968) found that the weights were a function of the corresponding backlog-expenditures ratio. Using her original lag estimation method, she found that internal funds and the accelerator mechanism were significant determinants of appropriations but that 'several other financial variables tested—the debt-asset ratio, the ratio of debt minus cash flow to assets, and stock prices—were not very useful for explaining appropriations.'[47]

In a similar study, Kareken and Solow (1963) identified the end of the first stage with data on new orders. They explained new orders using two alternative formulations: (i) a capital stock adjustment model with current profits and bond yield; and (ii) an ad hoc relationship including current output, profits and bond yield. The two formulations were first estimated on the assumption that the influence of the explanatory variables on new orders was immediate, though the second was then extended to allow for distributed lag effects. The transmission of new orders into actual production of capital equipment was studied, but without making any allowance for the variation in production periods through time. Kareken and Solow found that the percentage of new orders transmitted into production (on average) after 3, 6, 9, 12 and 15 months was 17, 31, 42, 53 and 61% respectively.[48]

There are two sources of aggregate ex ante data on investment in the United Kingdom. Beginning in July 1955, the Board of Trade has conducted sample surveys of the investment intentions of three subsections of the private sector; manufacturing, distributive and service trades, and shipping. Since its introduction, the scope and coverage of the survey has been gradually extended so that by 1967 it included about 4,300 business units. These accounted for about 60% of the private capital expenditure in manufacturing; about 30% of that in the distributive, and services trades; and almost all of that in shipping. Firms are asked to give three quantitative forecasts of their investment intentions for each calendar year: these are required in the preceding August/September, the preceding November/December and the actual August/September. Other non-quantitative inquiries are conducted before the first and between the second and third forecasts. A preliminary forecast is also sought for in the November/December twelve months before the beginning of the forecast year. The publication of each of the quantitative forecasts takes the form of a predicted percentage increase in investment between the year prior to the forecast year and the forecast

47 Almon (1968), p. 193.
48 These percentages are arithmetic means of two corresponding series of percentages, presented in Kareken and Solow (1963), p. 30, each of which related to two alternative regression equations.

year. These percentage changes are based on a comparison of the current expenditure forecasts and the corresponding ones made a year earlier.

The predictive performance of the manufacturing industry intentions series over the ten year period 1957–67 has been examined in Board of Trade (1967). Although the basic expenditure forecast for each year has almost always exceeded the out-turn by between 10 and 25%, the reported percentage-change forecasts have had quite an impressive predictive record. In an earlier study based on 1956–62 data, Ball and Drake (1964) had shown that the predictive performance of the manufacturing industry series was better than that of the other industries and services sector series, but both were clearly superior to two naive models. They also developed alternative realisation functions for explaining quarterly private (non-dwelling) gross fixed capital formation using quarterly predictions derived from the survey forecasts. However, they reported 'the importance of the direct forecast as an argument of the realisation function and the relative unimportance of the plan revision variable (discrepancy between expected and actual sales) that has been used'.[49]

Beginning in February 1958, the Confederation (previously Federation) of British Industry has conducted regular four-monthly 'industrial trends' surveys amongst its member firms. Since the second survey the following question has been asked about investment intentions; 'do you expect to authorise more or less capital expenditure in the next twelve months than you authorised in the past twelve months on (a) buildings, (b) plant and machinery?' The replies are reported as the percentage of firms answering 'more', 'same' or 'less'. The sample of firms in eight industrial groups and the proportions in four (employment) size groups corresponded to the proportions of total employment in both these groupings. However, since June 1964 a specific weighting system has been used to take account of these factors.

The predictive performance of the replies has been briefly examined both in the National Institute Economic Review (November 1963) and by Hart and Howe (1963). The National Institute article found the simple balances (more–less) to be useful predictors of turning points; however Hart and Howe pointed out that it is not they but their cumulative sum series which should really be used for prediction. Hart and Howe were only able to construct such a series for the plant and machinery replies, and a comparison of this series with the official expenditure statistics led them to the following conclusion:[50]

49 Ball and Drake (1964), p. 245.
50 Hart and Howe (1963), p. 15.

'Because there is no lag between the cumulative curve and the curves of the official figures the F.B.I. series in this form has predictive value only in so far as it becomes available about six months ahead of the official figures and there is certainly no evidence that respondents are reporting on their expected authorisations. On the contrary they appear to be thinking of their actual current investment expenditure.'

However, even if this is true, the C.B.I. series is valuable in substantially reducing the time lag before knowledge of (even) the present situation becomes available.

5.4. Guidelines for Future Research

The major problem in studying aggregate investment is that associated with the time lags to which the process of investment is subject. As described in ch. 2 § 11, for any particular capital good being purchased by an individual firm at a specific point in time, the lag between the investment determining variables and the resultant expenditure is likely to consist of both fixed and distributed components. Aggregation over types of capital goods, firms, and time, not only extends and spreads the lag distribution but renders it flexible through time. The methods of estimating (implicitly assumed) stable lag distributions are liable to either criticisms of naivity or serious problems of estimation, whilst those which permit flexibility are particularly troubled by multi-collinearity and restricted degrees of freedom. The most fruitful line of approach appears to be that discussed in the previous section; to split the investment process into two sequential stages and study each separately.

Given adequate data, this latter procedure may be generalised so that each of the stages listed in ch. 2 § 11 is studied separately. Unfortunately the necessary information is not available for total investment; nor indeed could it be provided since some investment projects do not pass through all of the stages and the ends of the first two stages are not clearly identifiable. However, data on investment reaching particularly important points in the process is often available for particular types of capital goods. For example, in the case of United Kingdom investment, data has been published on the approval, and start and completion of construction of industrial buildings, and on the order and delivery of machine tools.

There are a number of advantages of studying investment in particular capital goods rather than in total. The lag distribution for a particular asset is clearly less complex and for most assets will extend over fewer time periods than that for total investment. This advantage is additional to that gained by being able to identify investment passing through more, and more clearly defined, stages in the process. Moreover, for a particular type of capital good, the variations in mean production periods can be estimated using the non-regression method described in ch. 4 § 6. Secondly, the determinants of investment may well differ between different types of capital goods. Capital goods differ considerably in their expected lifetimes, in the amount of planning and expenditure which they involve, and in the degree of future commitment which they imply for the firms purchasing them. The purchase of a single industrial building may considerably affect and shape a firm's policy and profitability over, say, the next thirty years, whilst that of a single machine tool may be viewed almost as a routine purchase divorced from long-run planning considerations. Given this contrast it is somewhat surprising that in previous studies disaggregation has been mainly by industry or firm. It seems 'a priori' likely that decisions to buy the same capital good by two firms in different industries are at least as homogeneous as decisions to buy two very different capital goods by two firms in the same industry, or even by the same firm. The apparently contradictory results reported in previous studies may be attributable, at least in part, to this lack of homogeneity. It is noteworthy that the study of Kisselgoff and Modigliani, which distinguished between investment in plant and in equipment, confirmed the 'a priori' expectations that the time lags are shorter and the influence of profits greater in the case of the latter. A further advantage of disaggregating by type of capital good is that investment in a particular capital good is statistically represented by a much less smooth series than total investment, and hence the ability to discriminate between alternative hypotheses about the determination of investment should be greater. The ability to identify separate stages within the investment process increases this advantage, since as was shown in ch. 3 § 1 the first observable series is usually much more volatile than alternative series representing actual investment.

The hypothesis that different factors are of importance in the determination of the demand for different types of capital goods has received empirical support from an econometric study of United Kingdom investment in industrial buildings and machine tools.[51] Using data for the periods 1948–65 and 1956–65 respectively, the regression analysis suggested that of the variables affecting the supply of funds, interest rates are relevant to investment in industrial buildings and undistributed

---

51 This has been fully reported in the author's Ph.D. Thesis, 'United Kingdom Investment in Industrial Buildings and Machine Tools: An Econometric Study', University of Manchester, 1969.

profits to investment in machine tools—a finding again consistent with 'a priori' expectations. Alternative versions of the acceleration principle and capital stock adjustment formulations were incorporated into the analytical framework as factors determining the position of the marginal efficiency schedule. The regression analysis suggested that of these, the most relevant is a capital stock adjustment model in which the desired capital stock is assumed proportional to output. Although it is difficult to quantify the 'highly volatile and illusory expectations' which Keynes argued influence investment, new orders for machine tools were found to be sensitive to expectations as measured by stock market prices. On the other hand, such expectations appeared to play little role in the determination of investment in industrial buildings. This is not surprising since investment in industrial buildings, which involves a large expenditure and a longer time horizon than investment in machine tools, is more likely to be 'coolly considered in terms of a realistic appraisal of capital requirements from the standpoint of long-term considerations of growth'.

Amongst policy variables, the pre-Corporation Tax system of investment and initial allowances was shown to have had no significant effect on investment in either industrial buildings or machine tools. On the other hand, variations in the basic rate of company taxation appeared to have been highly important. As undistributed profits were found to be relevant only to investment in machine tools, the influence of tax rates probably operates through the marginal efficiency schedule in the manner suggested by businessmen, high rates of tax deterring investment. This suggests that investment may be more successfully stimulated by a general reduction in company taxation than by a more generous system of specific subsidies to investment.

The relevance of interest rates, also subject to policy decisions, was somewhat less clear. The rate on long-term government debt was found to be useful in explaining the demand for investment in industrial buildings, but only during one sub-period studied, 1953–65. Neither this rate, bank rate, nor either of two alternative measures of the cost of equity capital was found to be useful in explaining new orders for machine tools. However, the difficulty of constructing satisfactory measures of either the cost of equity capital or the opportunity-cost of internal funds means that any conclusions about the influence of interest rates must be stated very tentatively.

The method described in ch. 3 § 6 was used to estimate the mean start to completion lags in the case of industrial buildings and the mean order to delivery lags in the case of machine tools. These lags were found to be subject to considerable variation, with the result that the flows of completions and deliveries were much more smooth than those of starts and new orders respectively. Regression analysis identified variations in the amount of work in progress and the subsequent rate of starts/new orders as significant determinants of the average lag experienced by buildings started or machine tools ordered at any point in time. A method was also described for estimating the amount of work done on the production of these capital goods,[52] and application of the method produced series far more stable than those of either starts or new orders respectively. As conventional data on investment relates to expenditure made either at the time of delivery or at stages throughout the production process, it seems that such data will not fully reflect the considerable variations in investment demand. Direct application of regression analysis to conventional investment data may therefore be unable to identify the factors influencing the initial investment decisions. That seems an appropriate, if somewhat depressing, conclusion.

52 This has also been described in Lund (1967).

BIBLIOGRAPHY

ACKLEY, G. 1961. *Macroeconomic theory*. Macmillan, New York.

AFTALION, A. 1909. 'La realité des suproductions générales, essai d'une theorie des crises générales et périodiques'. *Review d'Economic Politique*.

ALCHIAN, A. A. 1955. 'The rate of interest, Fisher's rate of return over costs and Keynes' internal rate of return'. *American Economic Review*, **45**, pp. 938–943.

ALFRED, A. M. 1964. 'Discounted cash flow and corporate planning'. *Woolwich Economic Papers*, **3**.

ALMON, S. 1965. 'The distributed lag between capital appropriations and expenditures'. *Econometrica*, **33**, pp. 178–196.

— 1968. 'Lags between investment decisions and their causes'. *Review of Economics and Statistics*, **50**, pp. 193–206.

ALT, F. A. 1942. 'Distributed lags'. *Econometrica*, **10**, pp. 113–128.

ANDERSON, W. H. L. 1964. *Corporate finance and fixed investment*. Harvard University Press.

— 1967. 'Business fixed investment: a marriage of fact and fancy'. In: Ferber, R., ed., *Determinants of investment behaviour, a conference of the Universities—National Bureau Committee for Economic Research*, pp. 413–425. National Bureau of Economic Research, New York.

ANDREWS, P. W. S. 1940. 'A further inquiry into the effects of the rate of interest'. *Oxford Economic Papers*, **3**, pp. 32–73.

BALL, R. J. and BURNS, T. 1968. 'An econometric approach to short-run analysis of the U.K. economy, 1955–66'. *Operational Research Quarterly*, **19**, pp. 225–256.

— and DRAKE, P. S. 1964. 'Investment intentions and the prediction of private gross capital formation'. *Economica*, **31**, pp. 229–247.

BALOPOULOS, E. T. 1967. *Fiscal policy models of the British economy*. North-Holland, Amsterdam.

BARNA, T. 1962. *Investment and growth policies in British industrial firms*. National Institute of Economic and Social Research Occasional Paper. Cambridge University Press.

BERGER, J. 1953. 'On Koyck's and Fisher's methods for calculating distributed lags'. *Metroeconomica*, **5**, pp. 89–90.

BLACK, J. 1959. 'Investment allowances, initial allowances and cheap loans as means of encouraging investment'. *Review of Economic Studies*, **27**, pp. 44–49.

BOARD OF TRADE 1967. 'The Board of Trade's investment intentions inquiry'. Paper submitted to an International Conference of C.I.E.R.T. (International Contact on Business Tendency Surveys).

BOOT, J. C. G. and DE WIT, G. M. 1960. 'Investment demand: an empirical contribution to the aggregation problem'. *International Economic Review*, **1**, pp. 3–30.

BRITISH NATIONAL EXPORT COUNCIL 1968. Britain's invisible earnings, the report of the Committee on Invisible Exports. British National Export Council, London.

CARTER, C. F. and WILLIAMS, B. R. 1957. *Industry and technical progress*. Oxford University Press.

CHENERY, H. B. 1952. 'Overcapacity and the acceleration principle'. *Econometrica*, **20**, pp. 1–28.

CLARK, J. M. 1917. 'Business acceleration and the law of demand: a technical factor in economic cycles'. *Journal of Political Economy*, **25**, pp. 217–235.

CONFEDERATION OF BRITISH INDUSTRY 1965. 'C.B.I. investment incentives survey'. Unpublished.

CORNER, D. C. and WILLIAMS, A. 1965. 'The sensitivity of business to initial and investment allowances'. *Economica*, **32**, pp. 32–47.

DEAN, G. 1964. 'The stock of fixed capital in the United Kingdom in 1961'. *Journal of the Royal Statistical Society*, Series A (General), **127**, pp. 327–351.

DE LEEUW, F. 1962. 'The demand for capital goods by manufacturers: a study in quarterly time series'. *Econometrica*, **30**, pp. 407–423.

DENISON, E. F., assisted by POULLIER, J. P. 1967. 'Why growth rates differ, postwar experiences in nine western countries. The Brookings Institution, Washington, D.C.

DUESENBERRY, J. S. 1958. *Business cycles and economic growth*. McGraw-Hill, New York.

DURAND, D. 1952. 'Cost of debt and equity funds for business'. In: *Conference on business cycles, a conference of the Universities—National Bureau Committee for Economic Research*, pp. 215–247. National Bureau of Economic Research.

DURBIN, J. 1958. 'The estimation of economic relationships using instrumental variables'. *Econometrica*, **26**, pp. 393–415.

— 'Testing for serial correlation in least-squares regression when some of the regressors are lagged dependent variables'. *Econometrica*, **38**, pp. 410–421.

ECKSTEIN, O. 1962. 'Discussion'. Papers and Proceedings of the 74th Annual Meeting of the American Economic Association. *American Economic Review*, **52**, pp. 351–352.

— 1965. 'Manufacturing investment and business expectations: extensions of de Leeuw's results'. *Econometrica*, **33**, pp. 420–424.

EISNER, R. 1957. 'Interview and other survey techniques and the study of investment'. In: *National Bureau of Economic Research, Studies in income and wealth*, Vol. 19, *Problems of capital formation*, pp. 513–584. Princeton University Press.

— 1958. 'Expectations, plans and capital expenditures: a synthesis of ex post and ex ante data'. In: Bowman, M. J., ed., *Expectations, uncertainty and business behaviour*, pp. 165–188. Social Science Research Council, New York.

— 1960. 'A distributed lag investment function'. *Econometrica*, **28**, pp. 1–29.

— 1963. 'Investment: fact and fancy'. Papers and Proceedings of the 75th annual meeting of the American Economic Association. *American Economic Review*, **53**, pp. 237–246.

— 1965. 'Realisation of investment anticipations'. In: Duesenberry, J. S., Fromm, G., Klein, L. R. and Kuh, E., eds., *The Brookings quarterly econometric model of the United States*, pp. 92–128. North Holland, Amsterdam.

— 1967. 'A permanent income theory for investment: some empirical explorations'. *American Economic Review*, **57**, pp. 363–390.

— and STROTZ, R. H. 1963. 'Determinants of business investment'. In: *Commission on money and credit, impacts of monetary policy*, pp. 59–337. Prentice-Hall, Englewood Cliffs, N.J.

EVANS, M. K. 1967. 'A study of industry investment decisions'. *Review of Economics and Statistics*, **49**, pp. 151–164.

EVANS, R. G. and HELLIWELL, J. F. 1969. *Quarterly Business Capital Expenditures*. Bank of Canada Staff Research Studies, No. 13.

FEDERATION OF BRITISH INDUSTRIES 1960. Memoranda of evidence submitted to the committee on the Working of the Monetary System. *Memoranda*, Vol. 2, pp. 114–128.

FEINSTEIN, C. H. 1965. 'Domestic capital formation in the United Kingdom'. Cambridge University Press.

FELLER, W. 1957. *An introduction to probability theory and its applications*, Vol. I (2nd edition). John Wiley, New York.

FISHER, I. 1930. *Theory of interest*. Macmillan, London.

— 1925. 'Our unstable dollar and the so-called business cycle'. *Journal of the American Statistical Association*, **20**, pp. 179–202.

— 1937. 'Note on a short-cut method for calculating distributed lags'. *Bulletin de l'Institut International de Statisque*, **29**, pp. 323–327.

Foss, M. F. and Natrella, V. 1960. 'The structure and realisation of business investment anticipations'. In: *The quality and economic significance of anticipations data, a conference of the Universities—National Bureau Committee for Economic Research,* pp. 387–404. National Bureau of Economic Research, New York.

Friend, I. and Bronfenbrenner, J. 1955. 'Plant and equipment programs and their realisation'. In: *National Bureau of Economic Research, Studies in income and wealth,* Vol. 17, *Short-term economic forecasting,* pp. 53–111. Princeton University Press.

Gehrels, F. and Wiggins, S. 1957. 'Interest rates and manufacturers' fixed investments'. *American Economic Review,* 47, pp. 79–92.

Glynn, D. R. 1969. 'The CBI industrial trends survey'. *Applied Economics,* 1, pp. 183–196.

Goldberger, A. S. 1964. *Econometric theory.* John Wiley, New York.

Goodwin, R. M. 1948. 'Secular and cyclical aspects of the multiplier and the accelerator'. In: *Essays in honor of A. H. Hansen, income, employment and public policy,* pp. 108–132. W. W. Norton, New York.

— 1951. 'Econometrics in business cycle analysis'. In: Hansen, A. H., *Business cycles and national income,* pp. 417–468. W. W. Norton, New York.

Gort, M. 1951. 'The planning of investment: a study of capital budgeting in the electric power industry'. *Journal of Business,* 24, pp. 79–95 and 181–202.

— 1957. 'Comment' on Eisner, R., 'Interview and other survey techniques and the study of investment'. *National Bureau of Economic Research, Studies in income and wealth,* Vol. 19, *Problems of capital formation,* pp. 592–596. Princeton University Press.

Griliches, Z. 1961. 'A note on serial correlation bias in estimates of distributed lags'. *Econometrica,* 29, pp. 65–73.

— 1967. 'Distributed lags: a survey'. *Econometrica,* 35, pp. 16–49.

— and Wallace, N. 1965. 'The determinants of investment revisited'. *International Economic Review,* 6, pp. 311–329.

Grunfeld, Y. 1958. 'The determinants of corporate investment'. Doctoral dissertation, University of Chicago. A summarised version is

— 1960. 'The determinants of corporate investment'. In: Harberger, A. C., ed., *The demand for durable goods,* pp. 211–266. University of Chicago Press.

— and Griliches, Z. 1960. 'Is aggregation necessarily bad?' *Review of Economics and Statistics,* 42, pp. 1–13.

Haavelmo, T. 1960. 'A study in the theory of investment'. University of Chicago Press.

Hall, R. E. and Jorgenson, D. W. 1967. 'Tax policy and investment behaviour'. *American Economic Review,* 57, pp. 391–414.

Hammer, F. S. 1964. *The demand for physical capital: application of a wealth model.* Prentice-Hall, Englewood Cliffs, N.J.

Hannan, E. J. 1965. 'The estimation of relationships involving distributed lags'. *Econometrica,* 33, pp. 206–224.

Hansen, A. H. 1951. *Business cycles and national income.* W. W. Norton, New York.

— 1953. *A guide to Keynes.* McGraw-Hill, New York.

Hart, A. G. 1965. 'Capital appropriations and the accelerator'. *Review of Economics and Statistics,* 47, pp. 123–136.

Hart, H. and Prussman, D. 1964. 'An account of management accounting and techniques in the S.E. Hants. Coastal Region'. Unpublished. (The results have been partially published in the *Accountants' Journal,* January 1964 and *Scientific Business,* November 1964; mimeographed copies of the report are available on application to the Department of Commerce and Accountancy, University of Southampton.)

Hart, R. N. and Howe, C. B. 1963. 'The F.B.I. industrial trends survey, a preliminary analysis'. Paper submitted to an international conference of C.I.E.R.T. (International Contact on Business Tendency Surveys).

Hayek, F. A. 1941. *The pure theory of capital.* Routledge and Kegan Paul, London.

Heller, W. W. 1951. 'The anatomy of investment decisions'. *Harvard Business Review,* pp. 95–103.

156 BIBLIOGRAPHY

HICKMAN, B. G. 1965. *Investment demand and U.S. economic growth.* The Brookings Institution, Washington, D.C.

HICKS, J. R. 1935. 'The theory of monopoly'. *Econometrica*, 3, pp. 1–20.

— 1950. *A contribution to the theory of the trade cycle.* Oxford University Press.

HOOVER, E. M. 1954. 'Some institutional factors in business investment decisions'. Papers and proceedings of the 66th annual meeting of the American Economic Association, *American Economic Review*, 44, pp. 201–213.

HULTGREN, T. 1948. *The American transportation in prosperity and depression.* National Bureau of Economic Research, New York.

ISTVAN, D. F. 1961. 'The economic evaluation of capital expenditures'. *Journal of Business*, 34, pp. 45–51.

JACK, A. B. 1966. 'The capital expenditure function'. *Manchester School*, 34, pp. 133–158.

JOHNSTON, J. 1963. *Econometric methods.* McGraw-Hill, New York.

— *Econometric methods*, 2nd edition, forthcoming.

JORGENSON, D. W. 1965. 'Anticipations and investment behaviour'. In: Duesenberry, J. S., Fromm, G., Klein, L. R. and Kuh, E., eds. *The Brookings quarterly model of the United States*, pp. 35–92. North Holland, Amsterdam.

— 1966. 'Rational distributed lag functions'. *Econometrica*, 34, pp. 135–149.

— 1967. 'The theory of investment behaviour'. In: Ferber, R., ed., *Determinants of investment behaviour. A conference of the Universities–National Bureau Committee for Economic Research*, pp. 129–155. National Bureau of Economic Research, New York.

— and SIEBERT, C. D. 1967. 'A comparison of alternative theories of corporate investment behaviour'. *American Economic Review*, 58, pp. 681–712.

— and STEPHENSON, J. A. 1967a. 'Investment behaviour in U.S. manufacturing, 1947–1960'. *Econometrica*, 35, pp. 169–220.

— and STEPHENSON, J. A. 1967b. 'The time structure of investment behaviour in United States manufacturing, 1947–1960'. *Review of Economics and Statistics*, 49, pp. 16–27.

KADIYALA, K. R. 1968. 'A transformation used to circumvent the problem of autocorrelation'. *Econometrica*, 36, pp. 93–96.

KAREKEN, J. H. 1968. 'Monetary policy'. In: Caves, R. E., ed., *Britain's economic prospects, a Brookings Institution study*, pp. 68–103. George Allen and Unwin, London.

KAREKEN, J. and SOLOW, R. M. 1963. 'Lags in monetary policy', Part I in Ando, A., Cary Brown, E., Solow, R. M. and Kareken, J., 'Lags in fiscal and monetary Policy'. In: *Commission on Money and Credit, stabilization policies*, pp. 1–163. Prentice Hall, Englewood Cliffs, N.J.

KEYNES, J. M. 1936. *The general theory of employment, interest and money.* Macmillan, London.

KISSELGOFF, A. and MODIGLIANI, F. 1957. 'Private investment in the electric power industry and the acceleration principle'. *Review of Economics and Statistics*, 39, pp. 363–379.

KLEIN, L. R. 1950. 'Economic fluctuations in the United States, 1921–1941'. *Cowles Commission Monograph*, 11, John Wiley, New York.

— 1951. 'Studies in investment behaviour'. In: *Conference on business cycles, a conference of the Universities—National Bureau Committee for Economic Research*, pp. 233–277. National Bureau of Economic Research, New York.

— 1958. 'The estimation of distributed lags'. *Econometrica*, 26, pp. 553–565.

— 1966. 'The Keynesian revolution' (2nd edition). Macmillan, New York.

— BALL, R. J., HAZELWOOD, A. and VANDOME, P. 1961. *An econometric mode of the United Kingdom.* Basil Blackwell, Oxford.

— and GOLDBERGER, A. S. 1955. *An econometric model of the United States 1929–1952.* North-Holland, Amsterdam.

— and PRESTON, R. S. 1967. 'Some new results in the measurement of capacity utilisation'. *American Economic Review*, 57, pp. 34–58

— and SUMMERS, R. 1966. *The Wharton index of capacity utilization.* University of Pennsylvania.

KMENTA, J. and WILLIAMSON, J. G. 1966. 'Determinants of investment behaviour: United States railroads, 1872–1941.' *Review of Economics and Statistics,* **48,** pp. 172–181.

KNOX, A. D. 1952. 'The acceleration principle and the theory of investment: a survey'. *Economica,* **19,** pp. 269–297.

KOYCK, L. M. 1954. *Distributed lags and investment analysis.* North-Holland, Amsterdam.

KUH, E. 1963a. 'Theory and institutions in the study of investment behaviour'. Papers and proceedings of the 75th annual meeting of the American Economic Association. *American Economic Review,* **53,** pp. 260–268.

— 1963b. *Capital stock growth: a micro-econometric approach.* North-Holland, Amsterdam.

KUZNETS, S. 1935. 'Relation between capital goods and finished products in the business cycle'. In: *Economic essays in honor of Wesley Clair Mitchell,* pp. 209–269. Columbia University Press, New York.

LANGE, O. 1938. 'The rate of interest and the optimum propensity to consume'. *Economica,* **5,** pp. 12–32.

LEWIS, W. A. 1961. 'Depreciation and obsolescence as factors in costing'. In: Meij, J. L., ed., *Depreciation and replacement policy,* pp. 15–45. North-Holland, Amsterdam.

LINTNER, J. 1956. 'Distribution of incomes of corporations among dividends, retained earnings and taxes'. Papers and proceedings of the 68th annual meeting of the American Economic Association. *American Economic Review,* **46,** pp. 97–113.

— 1967. 'Corporation finance: risk and investment'. In: Ferber, R., ed., *Determinants of investment behaviour. A conference of the Universities—National Bureau Committee for Economic Research,* pp. 215–254. National Bureau of Economic Research, New York.

LIU, T.-C. and CHANG, C.-G. 1950. 'Consumption and investment propensities: prewar and postwar, U.S.'. *American Economic Review,* **40,** pp. 565–582.

LIVIATAN, N. 1963. 'Consistent estimation of distributed lags'. *International Economic Review,* **4,** pp. 44–52.

LONDON AND CAMBRIDGE ECONOMIC SERVICE 1967. *The British economy: key statistics,* 1900–1966. The Times Publishing Company, London.

LONG, C. D. 1940. *Building cycles and the theory of investment.* Princeton University Press.

LUND, P. J. 1967. 'Building statistics: construction times and a measure of work done'. *Manchester School,* **35,** pp. 257–275.

— and HOLDEN, K. 1968. 'An econometric study of private sector gross fixed capital formation in the United Kingdom, 1923–38'. *Oxford Economic Papers,* **20,** pp. 56–73.

MACK, R. P. 1941. *The flow of business funds and consumer purchasing power.* Columbia University Press, New York.

MACKINTOSH, A. S. 1963. *The development of firms.* Cambridge University Press.

MADANSKY, A. 1959. 'The fitting of straight lines when both variables are subject to error'. *Journal of the American Statistical Association,* **54,** pp. 173–205.

MALINVAUD, E. 1961. 'The estimation of distributed lags: a comment'. *Econometrica,* **29,** pp. 430–433.

— 1966. *Statistical methods of econometrics.* North Holland, Amsterdam.

MANNE, A. S. 1945. 'Some notes on the acceleration principle.' *Review of Economics and Statistics,* **27,** pp. 93–99.

MARRIS, R. 1964. *The economic theory of 'managerial' capitalism.* Macmillan, London.

MAYER, T. 1953. *Input lead time for capital coefficients.* U.S. Bureau of Mines, Inter-Industry Research Item, 52, Washington, D.C.

MAYER, T. 1958. 'The inflexibility of monetary policy'. *Review of Economics and Statistics*, **40**, pp. 358–374.

— 1960. 'Plant and equipment lead times'. *Journal of Business*, **33**, pp. 127–132.

MEADE, J. E. and ANDREWS, P. W. S. 'Summary of replies to questions on effects of interest rates'. *Oxford Economic Papers*, **1**, pp. 14–31.

MERRETT, A. J. and SYKES, A. 1963. *The finance and analysis of capital projects*. Longmans Green, London.

— — 1966. *Capital budgeting and company finance*. Longmans Green, London.

MEYER, J. R. and GLAUBER, R. R. 1964. *Investment decisions, economic forecasting and public policy*. Harvard University Press.

— and KUH, E. 1955. 'Acceleration and related theories of investment: an empirical enquiry'. *Review of Economics and Statistics*, **37**, pp. 217–230.

— — 1957. *The investment decision: an empirical study*. Harvard University Press.

— — 1963. 'Investment, liquidity and monetary policy'. In: *Commission on money and credit, impacts of monetary policy*, pp. 339–474. Prentice-Hall, Englewood Cliffs, N.J.

MODIGLIANI, F. and COHEN, K. J. 1958. 'The significance and use of ex ante data'. In: Bowman, M. J., ed., *Expectations, uncertainty and business behaviour*, pp. 151–164. Social Science Research Council, New York.

— — 1961. *The role of anticipations and plans in economic behaviour and their use in economic analysis and forecasting*. Bureau of Economic and Business Research, Studies in Business Expectations and Planning, No. 4. University of Illinois Press.

— and MILLER, M. 1958. 'The cost of capital corporate finance and the theory of investment'. *American Economic Review*, **48**, pp. 261–297.

— and WEINGARTNER, H. M. 1958. 'Forecasting uses of anticipatory data on investment and sales'. *Quarterly Journal of Economics*, **72**, pp. 23–54.

MORGAN, J. 1957. 'Comment' on Eisner, R. 'Interview and other survey techniques and the study of investment'. In: *National Bureau of Economic Research, Studies in income and wealth*, Vol. 19. *Problems of capital formation*, pp. 584–590. Princeton University Press.

MORRISSETT, I. 1957. 'A note on the empirical study of acceleration and related theories of investment'. *Review of Economics and Statistics*, **39**, pp. 91–93.

NAGAR, A. L. and GUPTA, Y. P. 1968. 'The bias of Liviatan's consistent estimator in a distributed lag model'. *Econometrica*, **36**, pp. 337–342.

NATIONAL INSTITUTE ECONOMIC REVIEW 1963. 'The F.B.I. industrial trends enquiry', **26**, Nov. 1963, pp. 63–78.

NEILD, R. R. 1964. 'Replacement policy'. *National Institute Economic Review*, **30**, pp. 30–43.

ORCUTT, G. H. and COCHRANE, D. 1949. 'A sampling study of the merits of auto-regressive and reduced form transformations in regression analysis'. *Journal of the American Statistical Association*, **44**, pp. 356–372.

PESTON, M. H. 1959. 'A view of the aggregation problem'. *Review of Economic Studies*, **27**, pp. 58–64.

PHILLIPS, A. 1963. 'An appraisal of measures of capacity'. Papers and proceedings of the 75th annual meeting of the American Economic Association. *American Economic Review*, **53**, pp. 275–292.

POPKIN, J. 1965. 'The relation between new orders and shipments—an analysis of the machinery and equipment industries'. *Survey of Current Business*, March 1965, pp. 24–32.

— 1966. 'Comment' on 'The distributed lag between capital appropriations and expenditures'. *Econometrica*, **34**, pp. 719–723.

PRAIS, S. J. 1959. 'Dividend and income appropriation'. In: Tew, B. and Henderson, R. F., eds., *Studies in company finance*, pp. 26–41. Cambridge University Press.

PULLARA, S. J. and WALKER, L. R. 1965. 'The evaluation of capital expenditure proposals: a survey of firms in the chemical industry'. *Journal of Business*, **38**, pp. 403–408.

RADICE, E. A. 1939. 'A dynamic scheme for the British trade cycle, 1929–1937'. *Econometrica*, **7,** pp. 47–56.

REDFERN, P. 1955. 'Net investment in fixed assets in the United Kingdom, 1938–1953'. *Journal of the Royal Statistical Society*, Series A (General), **118,** pp. 141–192.

RESEK, R. W. 1966. 'Investment by manufacturing firms: a quarterly time series analysis of industry data'. *Review of Economics and Statistics*, **48,** pp. 322–333.

SACHS, R. and HART, A. G. 1967. 'Anticipations and investment behaviour: an econometric study of quarterly time series for large firms in durable goods manufacturing'. In: Ferber, R., ed., *Determinants of investment behaviour, a conference of the Universities—National Bureau Committee for Economic Research*, pp. 489–536. National Bureau of Economic Research, New York.

ST. CYR, E. B. A. 1964. 'An empirical study of the aggregate production function for the United Kingdom economy, 1923–1962'. An unpublished M.A.(Econ.) dissertation. University of Manchester.

SARGAN, J. D. 1964. 'Wages and prices in the United Kingdom: a study in econometric methodology'. In: Hart, P. E., Mills, G. and Whitaker, J. K., eds., *Econometric analysis for national economic planning*, pp. 25–54. Butterworths, London.

SAYERS, R. S. 1940. 'Business and the terms of borrowing'. *Oxford Economic Papers*, **3,** pp. 23–31.

SCHUMPETER, J. 1934. *The theory of economic development*. Harvard University Press.

— 1939. *Business cycles*. McGraw-Hill, New York.

SHACKLE, G. L. S. 1946. 'Interest rates and the pace of investment'. *Economic Journal*, **56,** pp. 1–17.

SIMON, H. A. 1957. *Models of man, social and national: mathematical essays on rational human behaviour in a social setting*. John Wiley, New York.

— 1959. 'Theories of decision making in economics and behavioural science'. *American Economic Review*, **49,** pp. 253–283.

SOLOW, R. M. 1957. 'Technical change and the aggregate production function'. *Review of Economics and Statistics*, **39,** pp. 313–320.

— 1960. 'On a family of lag distributions'. *Econometrica*, **28,** pp. 393–406.

SOMERS, H. M. 1949. 'Public finance and national income'. Blakiston, Philadelphia.

SONENBLUM, S. and MAYER, T. 1955. 'Lead time for fixed investment'. *Review of Economics and Statistics*, **37,** pp. 300–304.

SPIETHOFF, A. 1902. 'Vorbemerkungen zu einer Theorie der Uberproduktion'. *Jahrbuch fur Gesetzgeburg, Verwaltung und Volkswirtschaft*.

STEUER, M. D., BALL, R. J. and EATON, J. R. 1966. 'The effect of waiting times on foreign orders for machine tools'. *Economica*, **33,** pp. 387–403.

SUMNER, M. T. 1966. 'A note on initial allowances'. *Scottish Journal of Political Economy*, **13,** pp. 352–362.

TAYLOR, L. D. and WILSON, T. A. 1964. 'Three-pass least-squares: a method for estimating models with a lagged dependent variable'. *Review of Economics and Statistics*, **46,** pp. 329–346.

THEIL, H. 1954. *Linear aggregation of economic relations*. North-Holland, Amsterdam.

TINBERGEN, J. 1938. 'Statistical evidence on the acceleration principle'. *Economica*, **5,** pp. 164–176.

— 1939. *Statistical testing of business cycle theories*, Vol. I. League of Nations, Geneva.

— and POLAK, J. J. 1950. *The dynamics of business cycles: a study in economic fluctuations*. Routledge and Kegan Paul, London.

TINSLEY, P. A. 1967. 'An application of variable weight distributed lags'. *Journal of the American Statistical Association*, **62,** pp. 1277–1289.

TUGAN-BARONOWSKY, M. 1901. *Studien zur Theorie und Geschichte der Handelskisen in England*. Jena.

WALLIS, K. F. 1967. 'Lagged dependent variables and serially correlated errors: a reappraisal of three-pass least squares'. *Review of Economics and Statistics*, **49,** pp. 555–567.

WHITE, W. H. 1956. 'Interest inelasticity of investment demand—the case from business attitude surveys re-examined'. *American Economic Review*, **46,** pp. 565–587.
WICKSELL, K. 1898. *Geldzins und Guterpreise*. Gustav Fischer, Jena. English translation is WICKSELL, K. 1936. *Interest and prices*. Macmillan, London.
WILLIAMS, B. R. and SCOTT, W. P. 1965. *Investment proposals and decisions*. George Allen and Unwin, London.
ZARNOWITZ, V. 1962. 'Unfilled orders, price changes and business fluctuations'. *The Review of Economics and Statistics*, **44,** pp. 367–394.
ZELLNER, A. and GEISEL, M. S. 1968. 'Analysis of distributed lag models with applications to consumption function estimation'. Paper presented to European Meeting on Statistics, Econometrics and Management Science, Amsterdam, 2–7 September, 1968.

Official Publications

BOARD OF INLAND REVENUE 1963. 'Income tax: allowances for capital expenditure on machinery or plant'. No. 430.
CENTRAL STATISTICAL OFFICE 1968. *National accounts statistics: sources and methods*. H.M.S.O., London.
ECONOMIC TRENDS, 102, April 1962. 'Income and finance of quoted companies, 1949–1960, pp. ii–xvii. H.M.S.O., London.
— 115, May 1963. 'Capital expenditure of manufacturing industry', pp. i–iv. H.M.S.O., London.
— 136, Feb. 1965. 'Non-quoted companies and their finance', pp. ii–xv. H.M.S.O., London.
Investment Incentives, Cmnd. 2874. 1966. H.M.S.O., London.
NATIONAL ECONOMIC DEVELOPMENT COUNCIL 1965. *Investment in machine tools*. H.M.S.O., London.
REPORT OF COMMITTEE ON TAXATION OF TRADING PROFITS, Cmnd. 8189, 1951. H.M.S.O., London.
ROYAL COMMISSION ON TAXATION OF PROFITS AND INCOME, 1955. *Final Report*, Cmnd. 9474. H.M.S.O., London.
UNITED NATIONS 1964. *A system of national accounts and supporting tables*. United Nations, New York.

AUTHOR INDEX

SUBJECT INDEX